NORTH AMERICA

BY

WOLFGANG HABERLAND

TRANSLATED BY WAYNE DYNES

METHUEN — LONDON

Title-page: Carved whale vertebra depicting a killer whale. Following the *pars pro toto* principle only the most important parts are shown: the broad, toothy mouth, round eyes and large dorsal fins, featured twice in the side flanges. Haida. *Width 34.8 cm. Musée de l'Homme, Paris. Cf. pp. 58, 59.*

*Dedicated to my wife Hanna, whose enthusiasm
for ethnology and art encouraged me to write this book*

CONTENTS

LIST OF COLOUR PLATES

LIST OF FIGURES

The line drawings were prepared by Dascha Detering, Hamburg.

FOREWORD

When the subject of American Indian art is brought up, the mind's eye responds almost automatically by focusing on Peru and Mexico, which are world famous for their early art and architecture. Those who are more familiar with the subject may enlarge their perspective to include Ecuador, Colombia and southern Central America. All these areas taken together encompass the area Americanists now call 'Nuclear America', considered to be the cradle of the Indian higher cultures or civilizations. Rarely, however, is attention extended farther north, where the imagination of many Europeans depicts the indigenous people as mounted bison hunters with war-whoops and trailing war bonnets. This idea, originally generated by early news reporting in the second half of the last century and later widely diffused by films and television, is most unjust to the North American Indian. Another reason may lie in the fact that European scholars, archaeologists as well as ethnologists, have been preoccupied with the study of the ancient cultures of Latin America, but rarely of those of North America as defined throughout this book, i.e. north of the Rio Grande. Thus it happens that books written by Europeans on the pre-Columbian art of the New World generally either ignore the vast northern portion of the double continent or at best present it only very sketchily. On the other hand, a number of outstanding volumes have appeared in the United States during recent years, which present a selection of the best of North American Indian art. They show that in terms of artistic quality there is no reason to neglect the area of the North in favour of that of the South.

To cite only a few examples: the wall paintings of the Southwest are in no way inferior to those of Mexico; the sculpture of the Southeast easily stands comparison with that of Central America; and the wood carving and abstract art of the Northwest has no rival. Consequently it was a great pleasure for the author to learn that the publishers had decided to devote a whole volume to this step-child of art history. May it contribute to a more complete understanding and appreciation of this realm of artistic activity.

A word must be said about the colour plates. While objects of historical times abound in European museums, the archaeological finds are almost exclusively in North American ones. There, however, they occur in such profusion that selection is difficult. Two points have governed the choice of the plates included: (1) the format of the book and (2) the desire of the author to enlarge the amount of published material. Therefore, several very famous objects ordinarily appearing in handbooks on American or North American art have either been introduced as line-drawings or not at all while other lesser known, but no less remarkable pieces have been included. The responsibility for this and all other decisions lies entirely with the author.

Many colleagues, especially in North America, have assisted in the procurement of illustrations and have often given very generously of their time. Since it is impossible to name them all, they must be thanked collectively. Special thanks go to the publishers for their unfailing patience and understanding as well as to the translator for coping with his often quite difficult assignment.

Hamburg, August 1965   Wolfgang Haberland

INTRODUCTION

As mentioned in the foreword, the often accepted picture of the North American Indians as bison hunters is a deceptive one, for the hunters of the Great Plains represent a late development brought about by strong European influences and pressures. This stereotype also obscures the breadth of cultural diversity, which was present in reality in North America, as witnessed by the accounts of early Colonial history. This very diversity of cultures and cultural areas with their different developments makes it difficult to give a picture of Indian North America and its art. What is more or less homogeneous today was formerly fragmented into many separate groups, often overlapping and with vague boundary zones. Several schemes dividing North America into distinct art provinces have been advanced, such as those of Douglas and d'Harcourt. These, however, have never been fully worked out and in some respects are even inconsistently characterized. For our purposes they are unsatisfactory – especially when historical and sociological factors are taken into account. Other existing classifications depend primarily on archaeological and ethnological data and are, therefore, applicable only in regard to certain aspects. Careful consideration of these problems suggests a classification more or less analogous to that used by Dockstader in his book on the Indian art of North America. The main difference is that in common with many other scholars he accepts a division between the pre- and post-European periods. Since a real continuity is in many cases undeniable (despite some sharp breaks between the two phases), this division will not be emulated here. Therefore, the main chapter headings are as follows: the North, the Northwest, California, the Southwest, the Great Plains, the Northeast, and the Southeast. To these are added, as an appendix, the West Indies. This area does not properly belong to North America, but is a cultural dependency of South America. It is included here because it was not discussed in the volume in this series on Ancient America, and because sometimes influences from or upon North America are postulated.

Furthermore, two topics preface the above-mentioned regional chapters: the finds of the early period, which often spill over or ignore the later boundaries and attract general interest as the manifestations of the first human settlements; and the petroglyphs (rock paintings and drawings) which are diffused throughout the whole area.

As a result of intensive investigations – especially since 1940 – the picture of North American archaeology has acquired considerable complexity; many sequences have been identified and divided into periods and phases, complexes and foci. These divisions, their development and the links between them, are subject to unceasing review and modification. Although the resulting nuances are important for close analysis, they will, however, only be mentioned in our text when they are meaningful for art history or specific art objects. Therefore, the reader has to bear in mind throughout these chapters that our knowledge of pre-Columbian development in North America is vastly greater and that its presentation has been highly compressed. For the convenience of those interested, the more important phases and complexes are indicated in the chronological charts at the end of the volume.

I. SETTLEMENT AND THE EARLY PERIOD

Scholars today are certain that the human race did not develop in the New World; therefore the ancestors of the Indians must have migrated into the Americas from elsewhere. Asia seems an obvious candidate for their place of origin, and in fact the New World Indians do share certain physical traits with the Mongolian peoples of that continent. It is now generally assumed that the migration occurred in a series of waves extending over a very long period. Opinions about the date of man's first appearance in the New World vary between 40,000 and 20,000 B.C. It is thought that the Bering Strait, which is now only about 55 miles wide with a maximum depth of 170 feet, may have been dry because of the lowering of the sea level during the Ice Age. Thus there would have been a stable land bridge blocking the polar current that now flows through the Strait. Some geologists hold that Alaska and northern Canada were warmer at that time, containing an ice-free corridor that paralleled the Yukon River and continued on the eastern side of the Rocky Mountains. In these circumstances it was possible for small bands of hunters (who had moved from Asia to America in search or pursuit of game) to reach the vast grassy plains at the foot of the mountains. They ultimately arrived in the Southwest region of the present United States. The Southwest seems to have been the initial focus of attraction from which groups were later to spread throughout America. But this hypothesis requires further confirmation, for it may be conditioned by the imperfect state of our knowledge reflecting the specially favourable conditions of preservation found in that area.

Migration

Hannah M. Wormington, an outstanding scholar of early Indian cultures, has identified three main traditions in the early period. These in turn are divided geographically and chronologically into many complexes. The 'Palaeo-Eastern tradition' embraces the most important complexes. Common to all is the hunting of diluvial animals (mammoths, mastodons, cameloids, giant sloths, the eohippus, extinct bisons etc.), the making of lanceolate stone points for spears and javelins, and the knowledge of pressure-flaking. By contrast collecting was the predominant method of obtaining food in the 'Palaeo-Western tradition'; since hunting played a minor role, stone points are rare.

Traditions according to Wormington

Percussion-flaking replaced the pressure technique and core tools are common. Typical of the Palaeo-Northern tradition are prepared core stones, prismatic flakes and microliths.

Krieger's classification In contrast to this primarily geographical scheme, Alex D. Krieger has proposed a classification by stages, of which only the first three will concern us here. As the earliest stage he posits a series of complexes that in the absence of stone spear or javelin points commonly have only rudimentary, scarcely formed tools made of stone or more often of bone. Although it is not entirely clear how this cultural evidence should be interpreted, the hunting of big game seems to have flourished to some extent. The dates of the sites correlated by Krieger appear to fall between 38,000 B.C.—or somewhat earlier (Lewisville, Texas) and 10,000 B.C. (Santa Rosa Island, California). This early stage probably includes objects regarded as the first artistic expression of the early Indians: two big stone blocks transformed into crude human heads (a third is very uncertain). The site where they were found, Malakoff, Texas, belongs to the Southwest, which together with California has produced the most evidence for this still very controversial stage.

Palaeo-Indian stage Much more certain is the Palaeo-Indian stage, which Krieger divides into several cultures, partly contemporary and partly successive. Common to all are stone spear and javelin points, which often take the lanceolate shape. There are also tools for cutting and scraping. Percussion- and pressure-flaking made thin, well-formed tools possible. Three cultures are particularly significant. The Llano culture, flourishing primarily in the Southwest and the Plains, is characterized by Clovis points. Mammoth hunting probably had an important place in this culture, which is dated between 10,000 and 8000 B.C. The Lindenmeier culture of the Plains exhibits another spear point type, the Folsom point. Like the previously mentioned points, Folsom points are channelled, but in contrast to Clovis points they always show pressure-flaking. There seems to have been an economic distinction as well, for the main game animal of the Lindenmeier people (9000–7000 B.C.) was the extinct bison. Finally the Northwest was the home of the Old Cordilleran culture with typical Cascade points in the form of an elongated pointed oval. This culture flourished between 11,000 and 8000 B.C. Apart from these three major cultures, a good many isolated finds belong to this stage, but they cannot be meaningfully linked together. As far as we can determine, all the peoples of this stage were hunters. To judge from parallels in Palaeolithic Europe we should expect a considerable development of art. So far little trace of this has been found. But the situation may change, for the dating of New World petroglyphs—in Europe these make up the mass of art works—is still an unsolved problem, as will be seen in the following chapter. Apart from this possibility, up to now the only art works that can with certainty be attributed to this stage are a few simple geometric engravings on pieces of bone.

The next stage of early development (according to Krieger) is the Proto-Archaic, termed Early Archaic or Upper Lithic by other scholars. *Proto-Archaic stage* This is distinguished from the Palaeo-Indian stage by the appearance of tools for grinding vegetables. From the evolutionary point of view this can be described as a transition to agriculture, yet the real causes must lie elsewhere, even if a certain internal development was present. The inception of the Proto-Archaic stage coincides with the disappearance of diluvial wild life following a change in climate (and possibly hastened by excessive hunting). The gradual depletion of herds evidently obliged the Indians to shift to other sources of food, or rather to make better use of them than before. Plant gathering was not unknown in early times; if the available data are correctly interpreted, it was simply less important. The diluvial animal population survived longer in some areas than in others and varied geographical conditions gave rise to a broad range of environments in which plants and animals could develop. This created a complex situation not previously known —at least which has not been established by scholars. During the next stage this produced such extraordinary variety that a general treatment of the whole is impossible; however, the foundation of the characteristic diversity of North American Indian cultures lies in the Proto-Archaic period, beginning between 8000 and 7000 B.C. The end of the stage varies considerably according to special conditions in different regions; it ranges between 5000 and 2000 B.C. One can pick out various cultures, mostly regionally based, that differ in many details, especially in the relation between hunting and collecting. Particularly worthy of mention are the Desert culture in the dry areas of the Great Basin, the Plateau region and northern Mexico; the Plano culture in the Plains and the eastern United States; the closely related Aqua-Plano culture in the Great Lakes area; the still controversial 'Arctic-Plano tradition' in the north; and the Balcones culture in central and west Texas and north-eastern Mexico. So far no art works are known from this period, but the possibility of petroglyphs must be borne in mind.

In conclusion let us review the early period of North America. Three main stages should be distinguished. The first of these, the Pre-projectile

Point stage, is still much disputed and by no means certain; it can only be retained as a possibility. However, the other two stages, the Palaeo-Indian and the Proto-Archaic, seem to be well attested. The former was largely restricted to a diluvial environment, while the latter was suited to a transition leading from diluvial fauna and flora to the present conditions. In both cases dependence on the environment is of overriding importance. Man was not yet in a position to conquer nature: he was compelled to adjust to it. Note that the shift from one stage to another did not occur everywhere at the same time, so that while one whole district was quickened by the emergence of a Proto-Archaic culture, other regions where big game lasted longer continued to be dominated by a Palaeo-Indian way of life. At the end of the Proto-Archaic period foundations were laid for the flourishing of the later regional cultures that will occupy us after the following chapter.

II. PETROGLYPHS

Petroglyphs have been found in almost all regions of North America and the West Indies. They include rock paintings proper, that is images and scenes rendered with colours on cliffs, stones and so forth, and rock drawings, representations engraved in the rock by various means. These engraved effects may be realized by scratching, scraping, grinding or pecking. Both painting and engraving lend themselves to a solid or outline technique. Thus the means of execution offered a broad range of expression; the choice was widened by the use of combinations. If we add to this the factor of stylistic variation, the diversity is almost limitless. This bewildering richness may have something to do with the neglect that this branch of archaeology has for so long suffered.

The few available studies, mostly old ones, amount to little more than descriptive lists; they rarely venture into the realm of interpretation. The field is clogged, however, with a mass of pamphlets of little scholarly value. They range from the notion that petroglyphs were mere doodles executed to relieve boredom to the arbitrary application of a host of weird religious speculations; from their interpretation as maps of buried treasure or diagrams of astronomical phenomena to being regarded as 'decipherments' and proofs of the presence of the most diverse European and Mediterranean languages. By contrast, very little has so far been done towards a more exact explanation and classification of these North American rock pictures. To be sure interpretation is particularly difficult in the case of petroglyphs, which can only rarely be connected with other finds so as to permit a secure dating and classification within a single archaeological period. Often this can only be done with petroglyphs executed in an easily recogniz-

FIG. I – *Pictograph with concentric circles. Forsyth County, Georgia; now University of Georgia, Athens. Photograph courtesy of Mrs. Margaret Perryman.*

FIG. 2 – *Depiction of a bighorn sheep in the Great Basin Representational style. East Walker River site (Ly-1), Lyon County, Nevada. After Heizer and Baumhoff, 1962. Cf. below.*

able style that can be matched in other objects of the same region. If difficulties appear at this stage of study, further progress is usually blocked.

Nevada Heizer and Baumhoff's monograph on the petroglyphs of Nevada represents one of the few exceptions to the above statement. This work demonstrates what can be achieved by exact observation and careful analysis of a large body of pictures, but also how narrow the limits of justifiable interpretation often prove to be. Some 100 sites were available for this study. The authors were able to classify the material into seven styles, some of them limited to certain geographical regions. Two of the style groups are rock paintings, the rest drawings. One of the rock painting groups, Pueblo Painted, could be linked with the Southwest and dated between A.D. 900 and 1100, that is a period in which part of southern Nevada was occupied by cultures of the southwestern type. The other painted style, Great Basin Painted, and one of the rock drawing styles, Great Basin Scratched, are evidently very recent and may represent imitations of the other styles. Of the remaining four rock drawing styles three are very closely related in as much as they all involve pecking and are distinguishable only by

FIG. 2 style. Typical features of the Great Basin Representational style, which is confined to the south-west corner of Nevada, are bighorn sheep, quadrupeds, horned men, hand and foot images and kachina figures. This last feature points to the Southwest, as does the geographical distribution. The appearance of this style in various parts of neighbouring states suggests that it had an eventful history, which may be connected in part with a migration of the Northern Paiute, though

FIG. 3 it is not known that they made rock pictures. The Great Basin Curvilinear-Abstract style, which is diffused throughout the state with the exception of the north-east, shows as typical symbols circles, meanders, zigzag lines and snakes, while the Great Basin Rectilinear-Abstract style is characterized by points, intersecting lines and 'bird

FIG. 3 – *Petroglyphs in the Great Basin Curvilinear-Abstract style; from the vicinity of Meadow Lake, North-eastern California. After Steward, 1937. Cf. above.*

tracks'. The sites of this latter style lie along the south and west borders of Nevada. In contrast to the figural style, both of the abstract styles seem to belong to an older stratum of settlement. At present they are dated between 1000 B.C. and A.D. 1500. Despite their differences, the three styles have something in common besides technique: they appear almost exclusively in areas that are suited for the hunting of bighorn sheep, antelope and deer. Thus a link between these rock drawings and hunting is likely and it may be that they functioned as magical devices for ensuring success in this vital activity. But the meaning of the individual symbols is still far from clear. The seventh style of Nevada, the Pit and Groove, is restricted to the south-western part of the state, though it is clearly connected with the related technique in central California. Various circumstances of the finds suggest that this is the oldest petroglyph style of the region, reaching back to the period between 5000 and 3000 B.C. However, Pit and Groove work was done in California in historical times by the Pomo, whose womenfolk hoped that this would promote numerous progeny, and by the Shasta and other tribes of north-western California, among whom it formed part of the rain magic. These chronological differences can only be explained by assuming that we are confronted with a very old cultural element surviving into the recent past, though possibly with a changed function.

This detailed examination of Nevada illustrates the difficulties that surround the study of petroglyphs. Of course there are also groups that may be explained easily or that are peculiar to a particular district. In many cases, however, hardly anything can be said about petroglyphs and ethnological data are rarely available. Some Californian examples have already been mentioned. Another group is connected with the Luiseño and Cupeño tribes of southern California, where young girls concluded their puberty rites by painting red zigzag lines or rows of lozenges on stones; these images were interpreted as rattlesnakes. Among the Yokuts of the San Joaquin Valley and neighbouring tribes it is said that rock paintings mark the hidden repositories of the shamans' magic. The complicated polychrome paintings in the Santa Barbara area of California cannot be linked to any known tribe and their significance remains obscure.

Artistically the human figures found primarily in Utah represent a high point of petroglyph art. The earliest examples occur in caves in the Southwest together with remains from the Basketmaker phases. These are still rather simple and only later were they to develop into richly decorated and carefully executed ensembles covering whole

California

FIG. 4

The Southwest

FIG. 5

21

Rock painting in red pigment. This elk is one of the best examples of the expressive realism of the rock paintings of the upper Great Lakes. Similar motifs appear in other media of the art of the Northeast. Lac La Croix, Ontario. *Cf. p. 23.*

FIG. 4 – *Polychrome rock painting of unknown purpose, tribal affiliation and date; Painted Cave, Santa Barbara County, California. After Steward, 1937. Cf. p. 21.*

canyon walls. Typical of the figures of the mature phase are angular heads with eyes, an almost triangular torso, rich head-dresses, round shields and facial images held in the hands, which could be masks or trophy heads. An exact classification has not yet been made, but a connexion with the cultures of the Southwest is certain. The debate as to whether these figures incarnate kachinas or masked dancers has not yet been resolved.

The rock drawings of the Northwest Coast and of the middle Columbia River are closely linked with the art of the region as a whole. Here we find all the hallmarks of the Northwest Coast style; they need not be discussed in detail here. The same is true of the petroglyphs of the West Indies, where the style recalls that of objects in stone and clay. More problematic are the red rock paintings of Ontario in Canada, *Ontario* especially those on the Great Lakes. They are executed in a uniform figural style and show men, animals, hands and boats, together with PLATE P. 22 occasional abstract motifs. Some paintings reveal an astonishing degree of realism. Despite extensive research, scholars have been unable to find any final and unequivocal answer to the problems of dating, classification and meaning. The most likely interpretation is that they were made by the Ojibwa or other Central Algonquian tribes during or shortly before the historical period and that they are connected with the birch-bark rolls of the region, which employ a similar style to illustrate songs and magic spells. The present-day Indians can throw no light on these splendid paintings; as so often happens, they attribute their creation to mythical beings.

Despite many omissions, the foregoing survey should convey some impression of a branch of art which was very widely diffused in North America and which sometimes reached remarkable heights, as in Utah and Ontario. But a thorough scholarly inventory is needed before a truly satisfying account can be given.

FIG. 5 — *Petroglyph of a heavily adorned figure holding a shield. Pueblo culture; in a canyon near Vernal, Utah. After Steward, 1937. Cf. p. 21.*

III. THE NORTH

The Arctic coast of North America presents a jagged, indented outline contrasting with that of Siberia. This impression is borne out in particular by the numerous islands of the Canadian Franklin District. The close interlocking of land and sea is decisive for cultural development. This feature also appears in other parts of the American Arctic, on the Bering Strait and on the west coast of Alaska; it is missing only between Point Barrow and the mouth of the Mackenzie River. To the east, the coast of Greenland, which belongs to America archaeologically and ethnologically, is similarly fretted. To the west, the Siberian side of the Bering Strait and the surrounding islands must be included here as well for the same reasons. Thus the limits of the region to the west, north and east are clear. Much more complex and uncertain is the southern boundary: it parallels the coast at a certain distance, until at Bathurst Inlet it bends sharply southwards to Chesterfield Inlet on Hudson Bay. The northern part of Labrador between the Fort George River and the Hamilton River also belongs to the north. This somewhat arbitrary definition is justified by the fact that it marks the southern limit of Eskimo settlement.

Owing to the lack of any natural frontier the southern Eskimo region does not present the uniform type of landscape found in the northern part. Two main units can be distinguished: (1) the North American tundra, with Arctic meadows near the coast and heather tracts further inland, and (2) a northern pine region with occasional enclaves of deciduous trees, which continues below the southern boundary. Both types of environment provide the caribou and the musk ox with plentiful nourishment, but grow no plants suitable for human consumption with the exception of berries. The sea coasts are inhabited by great numbers of marine mammals. Both the rivers and the sea abound in fish; there is also a considerable bird population.

In historical times this region was the home of the Eskimo, the only **ARCHAEOLOGY** indigenous non-Indian people of the Americas. They differ sharply from their southern neighbours not only culturally, but also anthropologically, for they are more closely related to the Mongolian peoples of Asia. They are also the only American group of which a part lives outside the continent. It is understandable, therefore, that their origin, length of settlement in the New World and cultural development have been the subject of heated discussion. Only through the more intense archaeological research of recent decades have scholars been able to come to terms with these problems, though a final conclusion is not yet in sight.

Early finds If the migration into the New World really took place across the Bering Strait, one would expect that very early finds would come to light in Alaska. But apart from two still uncertain phases (British Mountain, Kogruk), which are characterized by a supposedly Old World Lavalloisian technique, no connexions are known. Moreover, the dating of the 'Arctic-Plano tradition', which is found at various sites and which is regarded as an offshoot of the southern tradition of the same name, is still uncertain, for many culture elements remained alive in the north long after they had disappeared in the south. Thus it can be shown that the obviously typical Angostura mouthpieces of the Plano tradition continued in use in Alaska until after about 1000 B.C. The first firmly established culture group in the north is the 'Arctic Small Tool Industry', which is found at many sites and whose best known representative is the Denbigh Flint complex. With specialized burins, microliths and side blades, this industry had (to use the terminology of European archaeology) a pronounced Mesolithic character. This may have been the matrix from which a number of traditions lasting until historical times were to develop.

Northern Maritime tradition The most important of these traditions—and the best known—bears the name of the Northern Maritime tradition. Its oldest phase is Okvik I, which is chiefly documented at St. Lawrence Island and on the Asiatic side of the Bering Strait, while only isolated finds have come to light in Alaska. The link between Okvik I and the Arctic Small Tool Industry is a weak one, probably because of a gap in the archaeological record, which may be filled by the imperfectly known Battle Rock phase from Cape Krusenstern. This on one hand shows close connexions with the Denbigh Flint complex, while its art, on the other hand, which is characterized by straight, deeply incised lines, may constitute an early stage of Okvik I.

By contrast there is little doubt that Okvik I represents a fully developed

Human head of walrus ivory. The advanced stylization suggests a classification in the Okvik II phase, while the engravings seem to point to the Okvik I style. Found in the Punuk Islands. *Height 8.3 cm. Nationalmuseet, Copenhagen. Cf. p. 28.*

FIG. 6

PLATE P. 26

and already quite specialized culture in which walrus hunting played an outstanding role and in which the Eskimos may have already begun to venture on the high seas in search of whales. The main material for the remarkable art works of Okvik I was walrus ivory, which was used to make moderately abstract human and animal figures. More important are the engravings on objects of daily use. The transformations of their linear shapes and their combinations of symbols are among the most significant aspects which distinguish this and the following phases from one another.

If these phases were not set apart by other elements as well, such as the functional forms of the harpoon heads, one would have to speak of differences, not of phase, but of style. Despite the contradictory results of radiocarbon tests Okvik I is datable on typological grounds and through connexions with other phases to the period around 300 B.C., or perhaps slightly earlier.

The style of the succeeding Okvik II phase developed from the engravings of the earlier style—possibly by way of a transitional stage. While strong deep lines with long spurs characterized Okvik I work, this new phase presents a variety of lightly incised single or double lines with small triangular spurs. These lines often form a chevron open at the bottom and surmounted by a circle. These circles also now appear in other contexts. The two Okvik phases are distinguished not only in style, but by many particular details, such as the form of the 'winged objects', the harpoon heads and the relation between flint tools and those of polished slate. The general mode of life, however, did not change.

The established living pattern persisted in the following two phases, Old Bering Sea II and III (beginning between A.D. 100 and 300), which represent a direct continuation of Okvik conditions. The dwelling type seems to be an exception to this, for the round house of the Okvik II phase disappeared, giving way in the Old Bering Sea II phase to a square house with a long, covered entrance tunnel. Engraving styles followed the approach established by the earlier work. Curvilinear decoration and numerous circles mark the Old Bering Sea II phase, while the succeeding style has an almost baroque aspect with bosses replacing the earlier circles. This development came to an end about A.D. 500.

FIG. 6 – *Human figure in walrus ivory. The relatively moderate abstraction and the style of the engravings place this piece in the Okvik I style. After Birket-Smith, 1961.*

28

FIG. 7 – *Drum handle with a human face, in walrus ivory. Okvik II style. Found on Little Diomede Island. After Collins, 1937.*

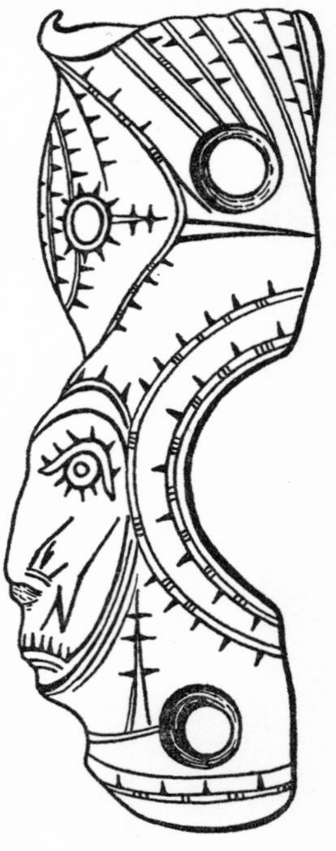

On St. Lawrence Island it is stratigraphically followed by a series of phases that are termed Punuk. Among the objects of the Early Punuk phase, several harpoon heads made of horn and ivory were found which more properly belong to another phase, Birnirk. For this reason it is often thought that Birnirk should be placed between Old Bering Sea III and Early Punuk, an assumption that is strengthened by the close connexion of the Birnirk style with the Old Bering Sea style. But to date no stratum has been found on St. Lawrence Island that can be attributed exclusively to the Birnirk phase, though pure Birnirk manifestations have been found, for example, at Point Barrow in northern Alaska and elsewhere. Therefore it is more likely that the Birnirk objects found on St. Lawrence, at the important site of Uelen near the East Cape, and along the northern Siberian coast are trade goods imported from the Alaskan homeland of this phase. On this hypothesis Birnirk was not a predecessor of Early Punuk but a parallel development. If so, there was never a Birnirk phase on St. Lawrence, but rather Early Punuk followed immediately upon Old Bering Sea III. Early Punuk is a transitional phase representing a certain break with older tradition brought about by strong influences from Siberia, as manifested, among other things, by extensive iron imports. Harpoon heads, knives and cutting tools could now be made of iron; the old flint industry disappeared. Other items, such as ivory link chains, seem to have been imitations of Siberian prototypes in iron. Nonetheless the fundamental 'Eskimo pattern' of culture remained and was further developed as, for example, in whaling. The new cutting tools produced a change in the engraving style, favouring an increasingly geometrical design with thicker and deeper lines as against the more delicate curvilinear patterns of times past.

FIG. 9

It is thought that about A.D. 900 Early Punuk changed into the Punuk phase proper, which lasted on St. Lawrence for the next 200 years. This is a period in which the previously acquired elements were consolidated and the geometric Punuk style reached its final form. But the way of life and the economy, which were conditioned by environmental factors, changed very little; they differ from the Okvik I phase of over 1000 years earlier only in the greater importance of whaling and the more thorough exploitation of fish and birds, which was facilitated by a new weapon, the bola with bone or ivory balls.

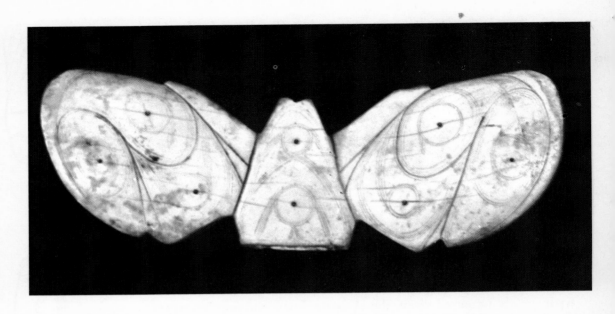

'Winged object' of walrus ivory. Scholars have long assumed that these objects, which are character-istic of the Northern Maritime tradition, functioned as parts of spear-throwers. But recent research suggests that they belonged to the equipment carried on the kayak where they were used to hold spears. The considerable modifications in shape and engraving make them a kind of 'index fossil' for the identification of various styles. Old Bering Sea II style. Found at East Cape (?). *Width 20 cm. The University Museum, Philadelphia, Pa. Cf. p. 28.*

The period from A.D. 1100 to 1500 represents a continuation of the Punuk culture and at the same time initiates another phase of transi-tion. The new influences came from the Western Thule phase, which flourished in Alaska; from it were taken over new types of weapons for hunting sea mammals. But the way of life underwent no radical changes during this Thule-Punuk phase except that the art of engrav-ing became sterile and slowly disappeared. After A.D. 1500 a gradual shift to the historical phase of the St. Lawrence Island sequence took place.

As noted above, the Birnirk phase, which grew out of Old Bering Sea III, initiated a parallel development in Alaska. On St. Lawrence, in default of other game, sea mammals became the main source of food. In the Birnirk phase the caribou (North American reindeer) was hunted—adding a new dimension to the economic pattern.

FIG. 8 – *Pail handle in walrus ivory. The bosses are a typical element of the Old Bering Sea III style. Found at Miyowagh, St. Lawrence Island, Alaska. After Collins, 1937. Cf. p. 28.*

Poorly fired pottery with curvilinear stamped patterns is another new characteristic which appeared for the first time. Chronologically, the Birnirk phase has been placed between A.D. 600 and 900, though earlier dates have also been worked out from radiocarbon tests.

Western Thule, which developed from the Birnirk phase, is the most important epoch for understanding the ethnological situation of Arctic North America. Although the two phases share many common features, the forms underwent some alteration, the tools coarsened, and the art declined. Note that toward A.D. 1000 the bearers of this Thule culture pushed eastwards as far as Greenland. Here, possibly under Viking influence, the Thule culture was modified in the thirteenth and fourteenth centuries. A returning current known as the Inugsuk phase brought the new elements back to the Bering Strait. Only through these migrations and cultural currents can one explain the uniformity that now embraced all the northern Eskimo groups between Alaska and Greenland. This uniformity is not confined to cultural matters, but may also be demonstrated from anthropological and linguistic data. The apparent gaps in the chain in central Canada may be attributed to the fact that in more recent times inland tribes (Copper, Netsilik, Iglulik) moved to the coast, where they replaced the Thule people.

The Thule culture, however, was not the first to penetrate into the eastern part of Arctic North America. Another culture had long been established around Hudson Bay, in Labrador, Baffin Land and Greenland. This Dorset culture, which is divided into a sequence of several phases that may reach back as far as 2000 B.C., was also an Eskimoid culture with a basis in the Arctic Small Tool Industry, as the very characteristic microliths demonstrate. The development, however, followed a course quite different from that in Alaska, possibly owing to greater dependence on caribou hunting. The Dorset people had, for example, no drills, women's knives or dog sleds. As usual in the Arctic, the rectangular houses built of stones and sod are sunk into the

Dorset

FIG. 9 – *Carving in walrus ivory of unknown purpose. Early Punuk style. Found at Miyowagh, St. Lawrence Island, Alaska. After Collins, 1937. Cf. p. 29.*

31

Ipiutak

PLATE P. 34

FIG. 10 – *Wooden carving with many slightly grotesque faces. Dorset culture. Found in the Upernavik District, West Greenland. After a photograph supplied by the Nationalmuseet, Copenhagen. Cf. below.*

ground with a long entrance tunnel. The art of this culture is typified by small sculptures in wood and ivory; the characteristic faces of the figures are often somewhat grotesque. The engravings seem much clumsier and more primitive than their Okvik—Old Bering Sea counterparts. What happened to the people of the Dorset culture after the Thule penetration has not yet been ascertained; in all probability they were absorbed by the new population, though no proof of this has survived in the material culture of the Inugsuk phase.

Alaska's most important site with its characteristic culture phase stands strangely isolated among the various traditions. Ipiutak in the Point Hope area is the biggest single settlement yet discovered in Arctic North America. This town had long rows of over 600 semi-subterranean houses of rectangular plan; they were made of driftwood with entrance passages and central hearths. Since none of the foundations overlaid any of the others, all the houses may have been in use at the same time. Food was obtained by hunting sea mammals (except for the whale) and caribou, the two being equal in importance. But differences from the Northern Maritime tradition involve more than the settlement plan and the food supply: the material culture, too, shows marked divergences. Missing are many objects for hunting sea mammals, as well as fish hooks, pottery, blubber lamps, bow drills, needle-cases and baleen objects. Although polished slate tools are also lacking, the stone industry was outstanding. The side blades inset in lances and arrows show that the basis for this culture is again to be sought in the Arctic Small Tool Industry. Artistically Ipiutak represents a high point unsurpassed by any previous Eskimo culture. Some engravings recall the Northern Maritime tradition, whereas others seem to point towards central and western Siberia. Small masks assembled from several pieces of ivory may have served as objects of adornment. Skulls, which were embellished with artificial teeth and eyes, are also typical of Ipiutak work. Still more important are the often very lively figurines of Arctic mammals in as much as they show the outstanding powers of observation of these hunters. These suggest a parallel with Scytho-Sarmatian art, a rapprochement that probably reflects no more than the analogous realism of execution. But connexions with Siberia can be proved, as the imitations of iron shaman's equipment and the use of iron engraving tools make clear. These imports suggest that the Ipiutak and the Early Punuk phases were parallel; furthermore, objects in the Okvik II style found at Ipiutak indicate that the latter must be contemporary with the Okvik-Old Bering Sea sequence, possibly with some overlapping in the Early Punuk phase. What followed this brilliant culture is a mystery: nothing has been found that points to a continuation of it. As we have seen, our understanding of Ipiutak origins is more soundly based. But here too there is a gap separating Ipiutak from the Denbigh Flint complex—a gap that might possibly be filled by the Battle Rock phase. Among the inadequately published Battle Rock objects is an arrow-head made of horn that is either identical with or very similar to objects from Ipiutak. The style of the Battle Rock phase and some other arrow-heads from this source are, however, related to Okvik as mentioned above. Thus it seems that both Okvik and Ipiutak developed from the same sources. How they grew to be so different remains an enigma.

Yet another tradition seems to have emerged from the Denbigh Flint complex, which begins with the Choris phase. With a radiocarbon dating of approximately 1000 B.C. this is one of the earliest cultures that can justifiably be called 'Eskimo'. The few facts so far known show that very different conditions obtained here from those found in the cultures we have so far discussed. The big semi-subterranean houses have an oval plan with the entrance above the earth's surface. Sea mammals were hunted, though they took second place to caribou in the Choris people's diet. Fired pottery with cord markings on the surface was in use. Slate was rarely employed and microliths, elsewhere so common among flint tools, are lacking. Thus there are important contrasts with the Northern Maritime tradition, contrasts that emerge also in the engravings, confined here to lightly incised double lines and points.

Choris

Norton

The tradition inaugurated by the Choris phase persisted in the Norton phase, which is found at Cape Krusenstern as well as on Norton Sound. This new phase accords more with the Northern Maritime tradition. Villages have sunken rectangular houses preceded by entrance passages. The caribou was commonly hunted but the stalking of sea mammals

FIG. 11 – *Human figure in walrus ivory. Dorset culture. Found at Iglulik, Canada. After Birket-Smith, 1961. Cf. p. 32.*

33

Small mask of walrus ivory with jet inlay. The several pieces making up the object were fixed to a wooden base. Ipiutak style. Found in grave 77, Ipiutak. *Height 17 cm. Nationalmuseet, Copenhagen. Cf. p. 32.*

increased and tools for hunting under the ice appear. With a few exceptions slate was worked in only simple ways. But flint was extensively used and stone served for dishes and oval lamps. Ceramics were more common than before and the potter's clay was tempered with sand. The art of engraving declined so much that it is hardly worth mentioning. Radiocarbon dates suggest that this phase goes back at least as far as the third century B.C.

The phase following Norton is called Near Ipiutak because the first *Near Ipiutak* objects were found in the vicinity of this famous site. In spite of this Ipiutak and Near Ipiutak share only a few common features and the chronological parallels are also quite obscure. It is, however, unlikely that they flourished side by side, for neither do they show traces of mutual influence nor (despite geographical proximity) do objects of one phase recur in houses and burials of the other.

Norton and Near Ipiutak, however, are linked in such a way that the derivation of the latter from the former, though not stratigraphically proved, can hardly be doubted. While pottery vessels and stone lamps continued in use, polished slate tools and characteristic whaling harpoons are new and must have been borrowed from elsewhere. In this tradition we are again ignorant of how later development proceeded from it. Connexions with southern Alaska—the district between Norton Sound and Bristol Bay—seem to have existed and certain features make it possible that the last group to belong to this tradition have been the Bering Sea Eskimos of recent times. The north-south extension of the tradition suggests an interesting hypothesis; if we equate Norton chronologically with Okvik-Old Bering Sea and Near Ipiutak with Old Bering Sea-Birnirk it seems that the north-south orientation of the Choris-Norton-Near Ipiutak tradition blocked the spread of the Northern Maritime tradition—an eastward movement of this tradition was only possible after this barrier had been broken. Following this hypothesis, we must assume that this happened first at the time of the Western Thule phase. Consequently the Western Thule people, unlike their predecessors, seized the opportunity to spread over the whole region. But proof of these conjectures is not yet available.

Finally a tradition must be mentioned that is associated with the *Pacific tradition* Pacific Eskimos and the Aleuts. Although certain artistic motifs and objects of material culture recall those of the Northern Maritime tradition, the differences between the two are noteworthy. Closer relations, however, are found with both the Choris series and Ipiutak— naturally enough, since both showed a southern tendency. The Pacific tradition is especially well known from Cook Inlet, where three

FIG. 12

phases can be differentiated: Kachemak Bay I-III. At the beginning of this tradition flaked objects of flint and slate are prominent, later yielding to polished slate tools. Kachemak Bay I is much more 'Eskimo' in appearance than Kachemak Bay III, probably because contact with neighbouring Indians from the south increased with the passage of time. This led to the emergence of certain peculiar features, such as whaling with poisoned lances, a method of fishing using harpoon points lodged in a hollow at the front of the shaft (in contrast to the northern practice of attaching them to a projecting peg), and the efflorescence of wood carving, weaving and painting. These characteristics have persisted until the present day among the southern Eskimos and the Aleutian Islanders. The Cook Inlet development is paralleled in the Aleutians, where the known material begins about 100 B.C. Whether connexions did exist with the Arctic Small Tool Industry cannot yet be confirmed, despite the presence of microliths in the lower levels at the Chaluka site on Umnak Island and other islands. This exhausts the more important proto-Eskimo traditions, as far as they are known up to date. Certainly many more will be added to them through further investigations, and some faint intimations of several new ones have been gained recently. One of them is the Old Whaling phase of Cape Krusenstern, dated about 1800 B.C. During this phase whaling, probably from sea-going vessels, was of the utmost importance. Besides the whale, small seals were hunted, but not large seals or the caribou. Further aspects of this problematic early sea-hunting culture include houses with complicated plans and several rooms as well as an excellent flint industry. The significance of this phase is still obscure. Certainly clearer knowledge of it will considerably change our ideas about Arctic America, especially in early times.

ETHNOLOGY

At first sight the culture of the present-day Eskimos seems to be quite homogeneous, but on closer inspection several sub-groups emerge, distinguished by differences of spiritual and material culture. First and foremost is the dichotomy between the coastal and inland tribes, a dichotomy already clearly recognizable in the archaeological material, for example in the Western Thule phase of the sites on Kotzebue Sound. Here jade objects, flint from the mountains of the Brooks Range,

Tupilak figure of painted wood. The mixture of human and animal features is well represented in the figure, which embodies and radiates evil. Angmagssalik Eskimo, Greenland. *Length 12 cm. National-museet, Copenhagen. Cf. p. 41.*

vessels of birch bark and other items attest to an intensive contact with the interior. Gatherings that can be described as 'trade fairs' also took place in historical times. Here groups from the interior and the coast could meet and in the nineteenth century even Siberian traders, particularly Chukchi, participated. We must assume that in prehistoric times too such markets (diffusing goods over a large area) existed. Thus a twofold division of Eskimo culture seems to have flourished at a fairly early date. How far back this distinction goes cannot yet be determined because of the meagre finds from the

interior. However, preliminary investigations in the area of the Seward peninsula, the Brooks Range and in Canada indicate a considerable antiquity.

These two main groupings of Eskimo culture were not in themselves homogeneous or uniform. The coastal Eskimos divide unmistakably into a series of sub-groups, each consisting of several tribes. One of these comprises the people living north of Norton Sound on the Bering Strait and on the coast of the Beaufort Sea stretching as far as Cape Bathurst in Canada. Closely related to them are the groups in Greenland; this link involves not only language and physical appearance, but also material and spiritual culture, both of which had developed on foundations laid by the Inugsuk culture. As has been mentioned above, another group of people who were originally living in the interior pushed their way to the coast, where they formed an enclave. They are called the 'Central group'. Finally, the tribes living south of Norton Sound in Alaska form a quite disparate group that at an early date—as the archaeological evidence demonstrates—followed a particular path of their own and came under the modifying influences of foreign elements: the Pacific Eskimos were influenced by their Indian neighbours and the inhabitants of the Aleutian Islands were subjected to stimuli from Asia. The interior tribes were also differentiated, though not so distinctly that they cannot be treated collectively.

Intensive investigations by Danish ethnologists have provided a most complete picture of the Greenland Eskimos which can be used as a model here. Rather than examine the whole culture, we shall confine ourselves to certain fundamentals and to aspects that are important for art. Nor shall we discuss the particular differences and nuances that characterize the three Greenland groups—the Polar and West Greenland Eskimos (both on the west coast), and the east Greenlanders or Angmagssalik. It is sufficient to say that because of the interior ice sheet hardly any contact could be maintained between the three groups and as a result considerable specialization occurred.

Greenland

Eye-shade of wood with decorations in ivory and puffin feathers. Shades of this kind were needed by kayak users as protection against the rays of the low sun. The ivory carvings show the typically Alaskan mixture of realism (walrus head, spirit figure) and abstraction (birds' heads). The engravings of the side pieces can be regarded as echoes of the Northern Maritime tradition. Alaska Eskimo, nineteenth century. *Length 28.5 cm., width 26 cm. Museum für Völkerkunde, Hamburg. Cf. p. 43.*

39

FIG. 13 – *Female figure in wood. West Greenland Eskimo. Museum für Völkerkunde, Hamburg. Cf. p. 41.*

Before the arrival of the Europeans, the hunting of sea mammals was the main source of food for the Greenland Eskimos, as was the case with most other groups. The best known way of hunting was with the ingeniously constructed kayak. But whaling, which was surrounded by much ceremonial, was carried out in the *umiak*, which held a number of people. The harpoon—thrown with a spear-thrower in Greenland—was used in both cases. Other objects of this highly specialized hunting activity include sealskin floats, wound plugs, kayak chairs and leather cords. Fishing was done with hooks or spears. Birds were hunted with bow and arrow or (among the Polar Eskimo) were caught with nets fastened to long poles. The rectangular winter houses of stone and sod were sometimes semi-subterranean and reflect house forms of the Thule culture and older archaeological phases. The frame construction of the roof covered with earth or grass is probably of European (Viking?) origin. Another traditional Eskimo device was the all-important entrance tunnel with its two skin-doors serving as air locks. The tunnel kept cold air from the interior, which was only minimally heated by semi-circular blubber lamps of soapstone. At night these lamps provided the only source of light, while during the day the room was illuminated by a window made of seal gut. Bow drills, women's and men's knives of various shapes, advanced fire drills, and bone needles with cases to contain them are among the everyday tools they used. Apart from the kayaks and *umiaks*, which were made of a bone or wooden frame covered with sheathing of leather, the Greenland Eskimos had sleds of various types, the bigger ones being drawn by dog teams.

There are great differences in dress among the various groups, but common to all is that it is the only clothing on the American continent which is fitted to the body and has sleeves and trouser legs. The fine skin mosaics formerly in use are now largely replaced by European fabrics and the big glass-bead collars have given way to ones made of lace.

FIG. 14 – *Small ivory figure, used by shamans as magic. The lip plugs are inlaid in blue glass beads. Found at Banks Island, Northwest Territories, Canada. After Dockstader, 1962. Cf. p. 42.*

Because of the necessary isolation in which individuals have to live, social forms have not greatly developed among the Eskimos. The biggest unit is ordinarily the family. A respected man was singled out as leader only when particular circumstances required the formation of a group. But this status was only temporary and never became a true chieftainship, an institution unknown among the Eskimos. In religion speculations on the soul mingle with concepts of natural spirits and the belief in a force dwelling in all things. Of importance are spirits resembling human beings which are deemed to invest certain classes of living creatures, natural phenomena or objects. Among these Sedna, the mistress of all animals living in the sea, enjoys the first place on account of the Eskimo way of life. Contact with her, as with all other supernatural beings, is maintained by shamans, who are assisted by personal spirits. The shamans also made PLATE P. 37 the Tupilak, found only in Greenland. This supernatural being is constructed from the bones of various animals—animals into which the shaman can then transform himself at will—and magically brought to life. The Tupilak always seeks to do men harm, breaking their implements and sinking their kayaks; his mere glance can be lethal. So it is not surprising that the wood sculpture of Greenland invariably depicts him in a horribly distorted form combining human and animal features. Wood was also used to make somewhat stylized FIG. 13 forms of men and animals. But this art, like that of the wooden relief maps, has disappeared. The ivory carvings which have replaced wood sculptures are generally made for the tourist trade. Other traditional craft objects, such as the lively engravings—mostly hunting scenes—on drill bows and boat hooks, as well as plaitings of coloured leather strips, are no longer produced.

As has already been emphasized, the members of the Central group *Central group* reached the coast only in late times, wedging themselves between two homogeneous units fringing the Arctic coasts. Despite their hinterland origin, their methods of hunting of sea mammals do not differ from those of their neighbours. In comparison with Greenland their economy is only modified by coastal ice conditions, which permit hunting on the open sea solely during the few summer months. Consequently seal hunting through holes in the ice is prominent, as it can be done throughout the winter; this skill has been brought to a high degree of perfection. The ancestry of these Eskimos is reflected by the caribou hunting carried out in the summer and the well-known igloos, domed huts constructed of blocks of snow that represent a further development of hinterland prototypes. The benches within and the ice windows, however, were borrowed from other cultures. In summer people here as in many other northern regions lived in tents made of caribou or seal skins. A special feature are the copper implements of the Copper Eskimos, who take their name from these products. As in the case of the meteoric iron implements of the West Greenlanders these objects were made by hammering the material in its cold state. But they did not reach the level of the finely pounded and polished stone implements. Besides line engravings, the craftsmen

FIG. 14 of the Central group shaped simple human figures of ivory. Recently under Canadian influence a new art has developed that is especially at home in Baffin Land and on the east side of Hudson Bay: iron tools make it possible to use stone, a harder material than ivory, for sculpture, whose subject matter includes activities of daily life as well as

FIG. 15 indigenous animals. Despite the apparent closeness to life, the Eskimo inclination to abstraction clearly persists in these sculptures. But how long this development can continue untarnished remains to be seen.

Alaska On account of common roots in the Northern Maritime tradition, the coastal tribes of Alaska and western Canada are closely related to

FIG. 15 – *Modern soapstone figure entitled 'Woman in the Wind' made by Akeeaktashuk. Craig Harbour, Ellesmere Island. After Canadian Eskimo Art, 1956. Cf. above.*

FIG. 16 – *End of a boat hook in walrus ivory. The engraved scene represents a walrus hunt from umiaks. Museum für Völkerkunde, Hamburg. Cf. below.*

those of Greenland. Changes and special developments are also to be found here. Thus the huge ice pack on the open tundra coasts of western Canada and eastern Alaska compelled the Mackenzie Eskimos living there to give up ice hunting. Therefore they developed whale hunting in the open *umiak* to such a pitch that they were able to obtain enough supplies to last through the winter with only occasional netting of seals. Dwellings were of various types, pre-eminently the rectangular houses with entrance tunnels noted in Greenland; the only essential difference lies in the construction of the roof, which these western Eskimos make from whale ribs. Houses with a central hearth, smoke hole and plank walls along the Bering Strait may have developed out of the houses of the Ipiutak phase. Among the many objects of material culture that distinguish Alaska from Greenland, the most salient are the pottery and eye-shades of kayak users. Art is especially rich in this region. As in Greenland, engravings on drill bows, boat hooks, net sinkers, knife grips and other objects of bone depict scenes of action, mostly hunting on water and land. Ivory figurines were used to decorate objects of daily use, which were often overladen with them, as for example, eye-shades and tobacco-pipes, the latter imported in recent times from Siberia. Human and animal figures, in whole or in part, provided the subject matter. Realism is more pronounced here than with the other groups discussed. It has already been indicated that southern Alaska, that is continental Alaska south of Norton Sound and the Aleutians, was quite distinct from all other Eskimo areas, and it can be proved that this separation goes far back into the past. The inhabitants of this region are set apart even in their hunting methods. Whale hunting was carried out with poisoned lances from an *umiak* equipped with a sail. Composite bows strengthened with sinews, elsewhere found only for land hunting, were employed here for sea-otter hunting. Another charac-

PLATE P. 38

FIGS. 16, 17

Southern Alaska and the Aleutians

Painted mask of wood. The mask, which is made up of many parts, shows the helper spirit of a shaman riding a beaver. Eskimo, Kuskokwim River, Alaska. *Height of frame 61 cm. Museum für Völkerkunde, Hamburg. Cf. p. 45.*

teristic weapon of this region is the bladder spear launched from a throwing-board. Although the mainland houses resemble those of northern Alaska with their central hearth, those of the Aleutians, which are entered through a hatch in the roof, point to Asiatic models. The plate armour and shields found in the Aleutians must also come from Asia. Great variations may be noted in clothing, which is based on a shirt-like upper garment that is often made of bird skin; since this usually reaches the ground, trousers are generally considered superfluous. Ear, lip and nose ornaments are more fully represented than in other areas. The Aleutian Eskimos wear wooden hats, which are often brightly painted; motifs found here and occasionally elsewhere seem to derive from Russian folk art of the nineteenth century. But painting is not the only distinctive feature of the many-faceted art of the southern group, for weaving and wood carving were also practised. By contrast, such traditional Eskimo crafts as ivory engraving and ivory carving are only feebly represented. Outstanding among the wood carvings are the death masks of the Aleutians and the masks of the Kuskokwim River. The latter often depict spirit helpers of the shamans, who use the masks to transform themselves into these spirits. All other Eskimo groups make little use of masks, as the rare flat leather specimens show. Sociological differences too set these Eskimos apart from the other groups: we need only mention inherited chieftainship and (among the Aleutian Eskimos) head-hunting and slavery.

PLATE P. 44

Finally the interior tribes, above all the Caribou Eskimos on the west side of Hudson Bay and the groups in the Alaskan interior lumped together as the Nunamiut, deserve brief mention. Ecological circumstances dictated a different way of life from that pursued by the coastal tribes. Caribou hunting provided the main source of food. The beasts were trapped singly in snares or driven towards fences in *battues* (mass hunts); they were shot with bow and arrow on land or intercepted from a kayak as they forded a stream. In mid-summer parties travelled to the coast to hunt seals and walruses and to take part in the big 'trade fairs', where the all-important blubber was bartered. Although other Eskimos possessed permanent winter quarters, these people did not, and so had to change their residence at intervals. In winter,

Interior tribes

therefore, many simply covered their tents with snow; others heaped it over a framework of branches, melted the inner surface of the snow with hot stones and left it to freeze again. In this way a firm structure was created that may have furnished the original model for the igloo of the Central group. The material culture of the interior tribes was often very poor and attuned to a nomadic life. Sometimes even the otherwise ubiquitous blubber lamps were lacking, but kayaks, *umiaks* and sleds were common. No special art forms developed among these people.

IV. THE PACIFIC NORTHWEST

The region

Anthropologists are accustomed to group the tribes living along the Pacific coast between Yakutat Bay in the Gulf of Alaska and Trinidad Bay in northern California as the Northwest Coast culture. The common features linking these tribes are not merely cultural, but also geographical and ecological. The Coast Mountains in the Alaskan panhandle, British Columbia and Washington State often reach as far as the rocky shore. Only in Oregon is the Cascade Range distant from the ocean, leaving room for foothills. Because of these conditions the middle and northern stretches of the coast are indented with numerous fjords and islands, sometimes of considerable size; the southern part has the only coastal plains worth mentioning. Despite its northerly situation and in contrast to the Atlantic seaboard at the same latitude, this coast is permanently ice-free, thanks to warm ocean currents. The same currents favour the rain-laden clouds that empty themselves on the Northwest Coast. All these factors combine to produce a predominantly cool and damp climate fostering an almost limitless mountain forest primarily of fir, spruce and cedar. Although wild berries provide the Indians with a modest source of nourishment, the land (except for the southern part) lacks any starchy food plants. Game includes bighorn sheep, mountain goats, deer, elks and bears; such migratory birds as geese were also hunted.

The Northwest Coast was settled by a series of tribes with the most diverse linguistic affiliations. Here we meet a phenomenon that will often recur in these pages: a relatively homogeneous cultural area made up of tribes of different language families. North America furnishes an excellent example of the fact that language and culture have often no direct correlation. Environmental conditions and cultural contacts, far more than 'common ancestry', have favoured the spread of prototypes and their firm establishment in certain regions.

Cultural development

The archaeology of the Northwest Coast is still little known. Not only have the few excavations so far undertaken given contradictory results, but the loss of perishable objects hastened by the damp climate makes interpretation difficult. Thus divergent theories have been advanced to account for the development in this region. However, the firm grounding of Paul Drucker's theories in ethnological data gives

them considerable plausibility and they will be used as a basis here. Drucker divides the tribes of the Pacific Northwest into four groups. While all possess the basic culture of the region, the individual groups reveal a series of special characteristics. Each of these characteristics may occasionally be shared with another group, but never with all. The main tribes of the Northern group are the Tlingit, Haida and Tsimshian. The linguistically related Kwakiutl and Nootka form— together with the Bella Coola, who are influenced by the first-mentioned tribe—the Wakash group. The Coast Salish-Chinook group adjoining the Wakash group to the south includes a number of smaller units besides the two eponymous tribes. The core of the southernmost group, in north-west California, is composed of the Karok, Yurok and Hupa on the lower Klamath; various lesser tribes complete this group. The central idea of this theory is that the Northwest Coast was originally dominated by a maritime culture that was very similar to that of the Eskimos with which it shared a common background. This type has been preserved in its purest form in the Wakash group. Later other groups pushed from the interior to the coast, overlaying this cultural base. They took over many ideas from the earlier inhabitants though without abandoning their original culture entirely.

Both language and material culture point to this conclusion. Thus the Tlingit and Haida of the Northern group belong to the Athabascan language family, which stretches inland as far as central Canada, and the nearest neighbours of the Coast Salish live in the interior of Oregon and Washington. Only the main tribes of the Wakash group —except the Bella Coola, who belong to the Salish—have no connexions outside their own territory. According to this theory, the settlement of the Northern group on the coast broke the direct contact of the Wakash group with the Eskimos, so that such later imports from Asia as rod armour were only taken over by the Northern group and are not found further south. The future will tell whether this interpretation can be supported by archaeological evidence.

In view of the surface conditions of the country an agricultural economy could not be successfully established here. Nor did big game provide a dependable source of food, for large-scale *battues* were only

Economy

Copper plate with engraved figure of the mythical 'Grizzly Bear of the Sea'. Tlingit, Queen Charlotte Island, Alaska. *Height 99 cm. The University Museum, Philadelphia, Pa. Cf. pp. 55, 59.*

FIG. 18 – *Limestone bust with eyes inlaid in abalone shell, one of the rare human figures in stone from the Northwest Coast. Haida. After Douglas and D'Harnoncourt, 1941. Cf. p. 58.*

possible among the northern California tribes. The northern Indians were restricted to hunting alone or in small groups under difficult conditions and what they bagged was not enough to feed the people. Unlike the situation in much of California (see the following chapter), wild fruits and vegetables were unsuited as the main source of food —except for acorns and camas roots among the southernmost group. The ocean, however, provided a plentiful catch—so rich that there was a real surplus. Here we find a sea-oriented culture whose emphases differ from those of the Eskimos; the main occupation was fishing, not hunting sea mammals. Salmon, which were caught during their seasonal journey to the spawning grounds, were predominant; second were oulachon or candlefish *(thaleichthys pacificus)*, smelt-like fish that take their name from the fact that they are so oily that they may be used as a candle when dried and provided with a wick. This fish was the main source of oil for the Northwest Coast. Apart from these two most important species, halibut, flounder, trout, herring and cod were caught in great numbers. Specialized equipment, such as the sieve-like candlefish net of the Kwakiutl, was developed for fishing. In streams the Indians used spears, baskets, nets and weirs; in the ocean hooks, harpoons and nets. Since most fish could only be caught during particular periods, it was necessary to conserve the accumulated surplus for consumption in lean months. Various methods of preservation were employed, including smoking, drying and pickling in pits. Candlefish oil was extracted and stored in watertight wooden chests. Only with the aid of techniques such as these could a sedentary culture grow up. The Indians' diet was supplemented by mussels, which the women collected, and by sea mammals. While men of all tribes hunted seals, sea-lions and dolphins with harpoons, only the Nootka on Vancouver Island engaged in whaling. In the latter pursuit the equipment, magical practices and many techniques resemble those of the Eskimos so much that they can be regarded as evidence of common origin. The boats used in all these activities were usually hewn from a single tree-trunk, but sometimes extra planks were added. The typical projecting bow and the high stern made them very seaworthy. Paddles, like the boats themselves, were often painted.

Houses Long rows of wooden houses formed shore-side villages, which the

Spoon of horn with bone attach-
ments. The engraved figure on
the lower part of the handle
represents a sculpin and the bone
attachment a killer whale, while
the handle end takes the form of
a bear resembling a man pulling
an animal out of his mouth. The
figure below may be a raven.
Tsimshian (?). *Length 41.8 cm.
Rietberg Museum, Zurich. Cf. pp.
58, 59, 60, 65.*

FIG. 19 – *Figure of a beaver. The typical characteristics: front teeth, tail and stick can easily be recognized. Part of a totem-pole model in argillite. Haida. After Boas, 1927. Cf. p. 59.*

Indians left only for fishing and hunting trips. The houses of the Northern group with their rectangular plan and sunken main room closely resemble those of the Eskimos. In the south this sunken main room was lacking, but two benches placed on the long sides gave a similar effect. While single-pitch (shed) roofs were preferred in the south, gable roofs were the rule in the north; they all shared a common principle in that the roof was not supported by the vertical pillars of the walls, but rested upon a special frame of posts and cross beams erected inside the house. Mat dividers partitioned the various living areas of the interior of these multiple family houses.

Materials From the objects we have already discussed, it is apparent that timber and other wood products like bast and roots played an outstanding role as basic materials. Probably there is (or was) no other American culture so dependent on wood and wood products; other materials —stone, horn, bone, shell, wool—were of minor importance. It is therefore reasonable to regard this as a wood culture. The intensive concern with this material favoured an extraordinary variety of techniques for working it, only a few of which can be mentioned here. The Indians took advantage of cedar's easy cleavage to make boards from it with stone hammers and wooden wedges; these boards were either used just as they were, for example, in house building, or kept as basic material for further carving. Rectangular boxes were made of thin boards bent over steam and knit closely together with bast or roots go as to hold liquids; they could also be used for cooking with hot stones. Water-tight baskets might also be made by weaving cedar roots. Cedar bast beaten soft served for capes, cradle linings, masks and clothing. Together with wool of mountain sheep (in the north) or of dogs (in the south), this bast was used to make fine blankets too. Since pottery was unknown, dishes, bowls etc. were also made of wood. Apart from wood crafts, basketry and plait work were well developed.

FIG. 20 – *Representation of a wolf following the X-ray principle. Painting from the bow of a canoe. Kwakiutl. After Boas, 1927. Cf. p. 59.*

FIG. 21 – *Wooden wolf mask. The angular style with sharp emphasis on the painting is characteristic of many art works of the Nootka, but appears with special clarity on wolf masks. After Gunther, 1962. Cf. pp. 59, 75.*

Among the products of this type are the baskets mentioned above and, especially noteworthy, conical hats. Moreover, blankets were actually plaited and not woven; the Indians of the two northerly groups let the cedar-bast warp hang loose from a cross beam and brought the woollen woof through by hand. In this way, to take one example, they made the famous Chilkat blankets, which will be discussed below. The Salish-Chinook added a second cross beam to which the lower end of the cords could be tied to make a simple loom.

Differences in social structure can be observed among the several *Society* groups. Thus the Northern group was characterized by a clan organization with exogamous marriage customs and inheritance in the maternal line. Among the Wakash group, however, the village society was the important unit and inheritance followed the paternal line. More important was the social hierarchy found in both groups; this class structure was also known in the south but was administered more lightly. Four social classes can be distinguished among the Northwest Coast Indians: chiefs (who never ruled over more than one village or clan), nobles, commoners and slaves (recruited from prisoners of war). The latter were not as a rule treated harshly, although they could in certain circumstances be killed. At first sight the chieftainship seems to be inherited, proceeding from father to son (Wakash group) or going to the offspring of the daughters (Northern group). On closer inspection, however, it seems (as with the nobility) not so much a matter of real inheritance of the chief's office as of transmission of privileges, whose combination led to the position of chief. The structure of these privileges was highly diversified. Disregarding nuances among the groups and tribes, these privileges generally included such dissimilar elements as heraldic crests, legends, dances, songs, membership in secret societies, titles, names, salmon-catching places, fishing and hunting grounds, the right to organize a whaling or hunting expedition and the right to harpoon a whale. The value of such privileges, which

FIG. 22 – *Man's garment in the Chilkat style made of cedar bast and goat hair. The pattern, which combines several principles of Northwest Coast art, represents a bear. Chilkat sub-group of the Tlingit. After Dockstader, 1962. Cf. pp. 59, 66, 73, 75.*

formed a kaleidoscopic medley of economic and imaginary advantages, varied from type to type and from tribe to tribe. For example, the two last-named rights were characteristic of the Nootka chiefs and were very highly regarded. Whoever held the biggest or best 'collection' of these rights was the most respected man of the village or clan, becoming what we call a chief.

The potlatch The titles and privileges did not become operative simply through inheritance; they had to be confirmed at a feast. As the potlatch, this feast has become famous in literature, where it is usually described in its late, excessive form. If someone wanted to pass on privileges—to his son, for example—he would issue invitations to neighbouring communities or chiefs. On arrival at the host's house the guests were carefully seated according to rank: the place directly opposite the entrance had the highest value, the ones near the entrance the lowest. The latter were generally assigned to slaves. When the proceedings began, the reason for the potlatch was announced, then the privileges of the host and (when appropriate) of the recipient were recited. The guests received blankets, which served as a kind of money; like the recitation they were intended to prove the wealth and power of the host. Thus transmission of privileges would be publicly and firmly established. Wealth could be demonstrated in other ways: by pouring oulachon oil into the fire and, especially in the Northern group, by ripping up the shield-like plates hammered cold from imported copper and casting the fragments into the fire or the sea. These copper plates functioned as a further measure of value in the semi-monetary system of the Northwest Coast; their value corresponded to the number of blankets which had been paid the last time the copper plate changed hands. The plates, often decorated with chased patterns, usually including the crests of the first owner, were so greatly esteemed as to receive names of their own. If they were destroyed in a potlatch of the Northern group, the owner had to bear the loss with stoic resignation. Among other groups they might be torn up and the parts distributed to the guests. But they were neither a gift nor a 'testimonial payment', for the guests were obliged to return the objects within a year with a 100 per cent premium. If they failed to do this, they incurred withering contempt.

PLATE P. 48

It is clear that the potlatch originally was a ceremonial handing over of privileges in the presence of witnesses linked to a demonstration of rank, rights and wealth. Business transactions might occur there as well. If, however, an existing rank was to be augmented, or even maintained, these feasts had to be interwoven with a whole cycle of events. Marriage, birth and death were events of this kind; others included erection of a totem pole, designation of an heir, conveyance of privileges to another person and entrance into a secret society. Still other events, of lesser apparent significance, might necessitate a potlatch, for example accidents befalling the chief that would be damaging to his prestige. In order to cope with such blows of fate a potlatch would be arranged to restore the host's rank to its pristine state.

Although the concept of the potlatch is familiar in general terms, we tend to conceive it in the form of a competition, that is, a series of feasts given alternately by two chiefs as a trial of economic strength,

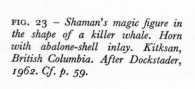

FIG. 23 – *Shaman's magic figure in the shape of a killer whale. Horn with abalone-shell inlay. Kitksan, British Columbia. After Dockstader, 1962. Cf. p. 59.*

the winner establishing his higher rank. The participants would seek to excel in showy feasts with a plethora of given or destroyed objects, which would be reckoned in blankets—whether the sacrifices were slaves killed, copper plates broken or boats smashed. The exhaustion of one of the two competitors ended this ruinous trial of strength. Since the prestige of a community depended on that of the chief, everyone felt obliged to help the competitor with loans. A defeat meant not only a personal setback for the chief himself, but a sharp loss of prestige in the eyes of his own community too, for the chief could not repay what had been lent him. This quite often led to suicide. This type of potlatch seems to be a late perversion of the original character of the feasts reflecting the stresses of the Anglo-American China trade in sea-otter hides, which produced a seemingly endless increment of wealth. Thus it happened that in the last quarter of the nineteenth century a great mixture of groups clustered around trading posts. Whereas in their original homes the hierarchy of the chiefs had long been fixed, at this time communities that had never met before began to come in contact. Normal friction was heightened by the fact that the ranks could not be reconciled into a single system and so, stimulated by materialistic influences stemming both from the Americans and the southern groups, potlatches were arranged to settle disputes. The full-fledged competitive potlatch seems to have arisen among the Chinook, who had two advantages that facilitated the transition: their position as trade intermediaries between the Northwest Coast and the interior (and later the Americans), and their custom of purchasing rank privileges.

Another aspect of social life must be mentioned here that also has religious significance: the secret societies, which flourished particularly among the Wakash group. The best known and most prestigious was the Hamatsa society of the Kwakiutl, whose initiation rite is often singled out in the literature. Like the potlatch and other ceremonial activities the admittance of new members took place in winter, a time of rest. For the initiates' father, who had to bear the costs for the whole lengthy ceremony, this was an expensive undertaking. But wealth

Unpainted totem pole. From top to bottom we see a hawk; a human figure with winged arms, probably mythological; a woman's head; a raven; a bear with a wolf and frogs coming out of his mouth and frogs from his eyes; a raven. Bella Coola. *Height 3.25 m. Museum für Völkerkunde, Hamburg. Cf. pp. 60, 62, 67, 70, 75.*

alone could not purchase entry into the society. Rather membership, as in almost all secret societies of the Northwest Coast, was an inherited right, which in the case of the Hamatsa society counted among the chief's privileges. The ceremonies were very complex, but essentially what happened was this: the candidate lived apart for a time in the forest where by solitude and fasting he worked himself up into a kind of ecstatic state. While still in the forest his personality was possessed by the Great Cannibal of the Mountain (Cannibal of the Northern Edge of the World is an alternative name), the society's patron; he became the spirit itself or at least an embodiment of it. While still in this condition, lured by rites, he returned to a house specially built for this purpose, where the festival guests and members of the society had gathered. Various means were tried to bring him back to his human state. This was the high point of the event, in which, towards the end, a corpse previously prepared by the initiate was brought before him and he symbolically ate it in the company of the other members of the society. This is the origin of the other common term for the society, 'Cannibal Society'. Without an exhaustive account, the symbolism and content of this part is hard to understand: but briefly put, the enjoyment of human flesh is something monstrous, something that no normal mortal would do. Yet the Great Cannibal of the Mountain is so horrible that, together with his assistants, who like him appear as masks, he eats human beings. When the initiate symbolically eats human flesh and in the course of the act tries to bite those present and when he symbolically tears up the corpse in this rite, he sets himself apart from other men and joins a separate class, a class accessible only to certain men. To belong to the Hamatsa society was a special distinction. Perhaps it is characteristic of the maritime connexions of these tribes that at the conclusion of the rite all members washed in the sea or with sea-water to regain their normal human state.

Despite the complexity of its outward manifestations, the religion of the Northwest Coast may be described as an advanced form of shamanism. As in other comparable religions, the magician-priests resorted to transformations and magic tricks; here their effectiveness was enhanced by such trick devices as movable figures. The shamans would also recover lost souls from under the sea. Among the Nootka the whale hunt was mimicked by a 'spirit hunt', in which a whale was supposed to be enticed to land by magical means. Apart from these shamanic practices, concepts of the soul were significant. These led, for example, to the custom of returning all salmon bones to the sea so that as living salmon they would return on their traces the next year. Similar cus-

Religion

57

FIG. 24 – *Shark split in two from rear to head and spread out laterally. Haida painting. After Boas, 1927. Cf. pp. 60, 66.*

toms surrounded other animals, which could be controlled by man-like animal spirits, the 'Lords of Animals', each of which was master of a certain species.

ART Social conditions of the Northwest Coast Indians have been described at some length, as their importance for art and its development is very great. In such a status-conscious society it is quite understandable that one should try to make one's privileges as conspicuous as possible. To this end crests, clan insignia and symbols of secret societies were applied to every kind of object. In the course of time imitation and variation produced an abstract, though lively art, which is one of the best known of any primitive people. Numerous scholarly books and articles on the art of the Northwest Coast Indians provide abundant material for study.

It is clear that distinctions among the groups and tribes mentioned at the beginning of this chapter are mirrored in art, and we shall discuss them later. But certain characteristics are common at least to the two northerly groups, and these, taken together, provide the essence of the art of the Northwest Coast; they will be explained first. There is no need to dwell on the fact that we are primarily concerned with an art in wood. As far as we can tell stone was a relatively unimportant material. Furthermore, carvings in slate, bone, horn and ivory are really only side-lines of wood-carving, from which they may be derived. A second important aspect of this art is painting, which was executed in various media. Finally basketry and weaving, particularly the

FIG. 18

PLATES PP. 3, 51

58

Chilkat blankets, must be mentioned as special art developments. In carvings animals were favoured above all else; as crests, as patrons of secret societies and as characters in legends they were held in high esteem. The animals were depicted in accordance with recognized conventions and each species had its distinctive identifying marks. These marks could be transferred to human faces or masks, which would then represent the protective spirit of the appropriate category, the lord of a particular species of animals. Only the absence of the otherwise essential big ears placed at the top of the head showed that men or creatures in human form were meant. Among the wealth of variations only the characteristics of the most important animal species will be reviewed here.

Animals

Three land mammals played a special role: the beaver, the bear and the wolf. Typical of the beaver are the two large gnawing teeth, the big tail with scales indicated by cross-hatching, the prominent round nose and (in complete figures) a stick held in the forepaws to indicate the animal's main activity. For the wolf the long flaring snout, the many teeth and the pointed ears trained back are characteristic. The bear has a broad muzzle with numerous teeth, the tongue often lolling through them. In profile view the sharp angle between the nose and the skull is striking. When the whole figure is shown a further characteristic is the big paws. Other less familiar land animals include the mink, mountain goat and otter.

FIG. 19

FIGS. 20, 21

FIG. 22
PLATE P. 48

Among the sea mammals the killer whale is the most important. Its hallmark is a prominent dorsal fin, which none of the other animals displays in art. A number of other features can be regarded as secondary, such as the big toothy mouth in the large head, in which the blowing hole is also shown. The eyes of the killer whale are mostly

PLATES PP. 3, 51

FIG. 23

FIG. 25 – *Sculpin with centre-split. Painting from a wooden hat. Haida. After Boas, 1927. Cf. p. 60.*

FIG. 26 – *Eagle. The individual parts are composed in the available space without reference to the actual sequence. Part of a wooden berry spoon. Haida. After Boas, 1927. Cf. p. 62.*

round, the nostrils large and elongated. Porpoises, whales, seals and sea-lions are also occasionally depicted, but the actual proportion of all these (taken collectively) is quite low.

Of the other identifiable sea animals two deserve special mention, sharks and sculpins, while halibut and octopus are rare. The sculpin is easily recognizable, since it has two features that distinguish it from all other animals: two vertebrae directly over the mouth and a long dorsal fin running along the whole body; this fin is often dentated.

PLATE P. 51
FIG. 24

The identifying features of the shark are a toothy mouth turned down at the corners, flanked by a row of crescent-shaped openings (gills). The head is always surmounted by a high cone, rounded at the upper end and in the shape of a shark's head, with crescent-shaped openings and sometimes circular decorations. When the whole animal is depicted, the asymmetrical tail appears as a characteristic.

PLATE P. 56

The frog with its broad toothless mouth and flat nose is easy to recognize and quite often depicted. Other reptiles and amphibians are not shown. Surprisingly enough even lower animals appear among the symbols and heraldic crests. There are even snails and mosquitos, though these are not too common. More frequent is the dragon-fly, which is unmistakable with its large head, slender segmented body and two pairs of wings.

Probably birds provide the greatest variation among the animal groups represented in Northwest Coast art. Apart from depictions of unidentified species, which perhaps only represent the idea 'bird', we find hawks, eagles, ravens, cormorants, geese, cranes and woodpeckers. Of these the first three are particularly important. While the beak and wing always appear in birds, different kinds of beak are

PLATE P. 56

especially important for distinguishing the several species. The beak

Club of whale bone with abalone inlay. The ornament on the grip end shows some characteristics of a bear as well as some of a thunder bird. Comparison with other pieces shows that the latter was the prototype. The piece was acquired between 1868 and 1871 near Fort Royal, British Columbia. Consequently it comes from Kwakiutl territory, though it must have been made by the Nootka who specialized in objects of this kind. *Height 52.7 cm. Provincial Museum, Victoria, British Columbia. Cf. pp. 64, 77.*

60

FIG. 26

PLATE P. 56

of the hawk is large and curves down so far that its point touches the head again. The eagle's beak is similarly large and bent, but here the bend starts only towards the end and the point is directed downwards. Finally the raven's beak is almost straight with the point directed forwards; often this bird can also be recognized by the ball it holds in its beak.

The most important living animals have now been mentioned with their characteristic features. Surveying the ensemble once more, it is curious how the animals that are most important for the maintenance of human life are largely or wholly missing. Salmon and candlefish are absent, not to mention other important species of fish, except for the halibut. To be sure, seals, sea-lions and whales are represented, though infrequently. The mountain goat is uncommon; deer and sea otters are altogether wanting. The same pattern prevails among the birds: the species that are *not* hunted are the ones most important for art. Scholars have advanced the explanation that the animals depicted are the ones figuring in mythology, for only these are significant for crests, legends, dances, secret societies. Thus they are bound up with the whole cycle of ceremony and ritual of which the art of the Northwest Coast forms a vital part. But this solution is not really satisfying, for it simply shifts the problem from art to mythology. Perhaps it is important that it is always predatory animals that play the greatest role, animals which can be regarded as enemies of man since they may reduce his catch. Sharks, bears, wolves, killer whales, eagles and hawks obviously belong in this category. Must man placate them in order to succeed in hunting and fishing? Can they transmit to man their own skill as hunters? Further research is needed to clarify this question.

Mythical creatures One more group of animals is important for art: mythological creatures. Almost all of these are endowed with traits of predatory animals and thus fit in well with the theory just outlined. Like all mythical animals they are nothing more than a combination of parts of various animals that appear as a whole in other contexts. Many of them belong to a

Carved and painted screen. Fixed wall screens of this type set off the sleeping area of the chief whose crest (in this instance a bear) was prominently displayed. In the photograph the entrance—in the animal's lower body—is shut. The principles of *horror vacui* and the eye-joint are conspicuously applied. The partially visible wings bear figures of ravens. From the house of Chief Shakes, Wrangell, Alaska. Tlingit. *Height about 5 m. Denver Art Museum. Cf. p. 66.*

FIG. 27 – *Argillite plate. The pattern, which is executed in scrimshaw-like technique, derives from European sources. Haida. Museum für Völkerkunde, Lübeck. Cf. pp. 70, 75.*

single category, the sea monster; it is often hard to distinguish the individual members of this group. One of them, the Wasco, is a wolf with the characteristic fin of a killer whale; thus endowed he is thought to be able to hunt on both land and sea. Another of these monsters is the 'grizzly bear of the sea', who combines traits of the bear and the killer whale. In this case the selection of components can vary a great deal. The two main types of representation are: (1) bear figures with fins on the elbows; and (2) bear's head and paws attached to the body of the killer whale, who in this case usually has several dorsal fins. The killer whale also provides part of the Tsum'a'ts: his upper body is joined to a raven's head and his dorsal fins to the body of the bird. The same being is also shown as a bear with a shark's mouth. While snakes are missing as such, they appear among the mythical beasts, either as the double-headed snake Sisiutl or as a lightning snake. In both cases the long body is covered with semi-circular scales. Typical of the snake head is a curved horn on the nose and a curved or curled

PLATE P. 61

ear. Another mythical animal is the thunder bird, very similar to the eagle, from which it is distinguished only by a tuft of feathers on the head. When the thunder bird is shown as a whole it usually has its wings extended. Finally the personified tree-stump Ts'um'os is the only object from the plant world to be represented in Northwest Coast art. Its form, that of a bear with a shark's head, strongly resembles a type of Tsum'a'ts.

This canon of symbols is very important for the understanding of Northwest Coast art. It permitted the artist to recall an animal merely by a feature or two instead of depicting it as a whole. This procedure is clearly seen in the masks, which otherwise show human features: through carved or painted symbols the masks are transformed into animals, or rather to the lords of the animal groups. A mask that has a beak curving down to the lip instead of a nose no longer represents a man but a hawk. The same principle was used in face painting as well, where a single feature might serve to suggest the animal (in other words, the clan or society) represented by the dancer. Thus it was always possible to disclose one's position in society and—since the prestige of the several groups varied, as we have seen—one's rank

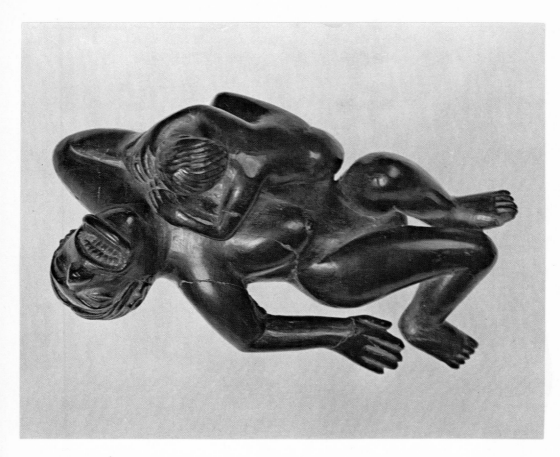

Argillite figure of the Bear Mother. Made by the Haida artist Tsagay from Skidegate, Queen Charlotte Islands, British Columbia, ca. 1883. *Length 14 cm. U. S. National Museum, Washington, D. C. Cf. pp. 69, 75.*

as well. All objects, especially those shown on festal occasions, had to display the crests and symbols appropriate to their owners.

This explains the extraordinary wealth of art objects from the Northwest Coast, as well as the range of variation in material and form. When feasible the whole animal was shown three-dimensionally—on totem poles, feast dishes, halibut hooks, the handles of spoons made of mountain-goat horn. On other occasions the artist showed only the head of the animal, as in the masks and wooden hats. But difficulty

PLATE P. 51

arose with the conical hats executed in basketwork technique. These did not readily lend themselves to the shaping of three-dimensional animals, so the beasts were painted. This painting had to be carried out in such a way as to assimilate the hat to the animal itself, that is the animal must be recognizable in frontal view as well as from either 'Splitting' side. In order to achieve this the animal's body was split lengthwise, as it were, and pulled over the cone of the hat. Thus the cone itself FIG. 25 remained empty, at least on the top, but the front, sides and back of the animal could all be seen. Strictly speaking the artist really painted two animals sharing a common head and tail (or rear part of the body). FIG. 24 Frequently, with mammals and fish particularly, the head was composed of two side views. This principle, which may have originated either here or in related objects, was applied to other surfaces, sometimes flat ones, including house walls, pieces of clothing and tattoo PLATE P. 63 patterns. While mammals appear as if cut from the back, birds were split from the breast. It must be admitted, however, that these princi-
Other principles ples were not consistently applied: there were many paintings and reliefs showing only a side view or a head from the front.

On the other hand three closely related principles were almost consistently used in painting and relief carving of the Northwest Coast: *horror vacui*, the 'X-ray view' and 'eye joints'. The influence of the *horror vacui* principle was very widespread, inducing the artists to seek to fill all empty spaces by repeating such surface features as hair, features and scales in painting and carving. Just as common, if not more so, was the second principle, the X-ray view, by which the artist segmented the body with parts not visible externally—the spinal column, the main bones of fish, or the entrails rendered in very abstract fashion. The X-ray principle was not limited to the body but was often used on the head as well, in which particular bones were shown. The third principle mentioned, the 'eye joints', is connected both with *horror vacui* and with the X-ray view. The joints, when they are represented, appear as eyes or concentric circles. Sometimes eyes are shown in such profusion as to make interpretation difficult, especially in a complicated and abstract pattern. On occasion, particularly with larger objects, the artist went even farther, replacing the eyes with

FIG. 28 – *Wooden figure of a shaman's helper spirit in the flat style of the Salish-Chinook region. Only the indication of the ribs according to the X-ray principle recalls the art of the Northwest Coast. Coast Salish, about 1899. After Douglas and D'Harnoncourt, 1941. Cf. p. 77.*

faces or even whole figures so that the image became even more unclear.

The general principle of *pars pro toto*, which has already been alluded to by implication, was employed not merely for masks and face paintings but for all those objects which because of their minor role or small scale were unsuited to representation of the whole animal. Since they did not feel an arrangement following the natural order of the parts to be necessary, the artists first placed the most characteristic parts of the animal on the available surface and then fitted lesser parts in the remaining corners according to the *horror vacui* principle. Not surprisingly, it is often almost impossible to tell what animal is meant by the fragmented parts.

The best known objects of the Northwest Coast are the so-called totem poles. They come almost exclusively from the area of the Northern groups, being most developed among the Haida. The poles might be set up before house entrances (in which case they were provided with an opening in the middle), at the corners of houses, in front of houses and over tombs. Although usage has established the name, 'totem pole', they might be more correctly termed 'crest poles', for they show primarily the crests and heraldic animals of the owner of the house and the community living in the house or, in the case of tombs, those of the deceased. Here too privileges came into play, since only chiefs and nobles might erect these poles. Apart from crests, the poles retold legends, sometimes showing how the first owner of the crest received it or how he came by some other specific privilege. It might be assumed that a knowledge of the conventions would permit reading off these legends from the pole. But the depictions on the poles provide no continuous narrative running from one end to the other. Rather the carver selected some separate incidents or figures of the narrative, presenting them on the pole according to his own aesthetic point of view. Thus the artist might evoke a whole legend either by a single figure, or by a series of images. Consequently the meaning of the whole composition is known only to the carver and his patron and cannot be fully interpreted by others.

How long the totem poles have been erected is controversial. One school holds that the poles were only set up after the arrival of the

Totem poles

PLATE P. 56

67

Painted mask. In contrast to the animal figures, the human images, especially the masks, project an extraordinary expressive power untrammelled by conventions. Northwest Coast culture (Kwakiutl ?). *Height 24.5 cm. Naturhistorisches Museum, Oldenburg. Cf. p. 70.*

FIG. 30 – *Head ornament in horn in human form, representing the severe style of the earlier period on the middle Columbia. The ribs are already indicated (cf. Fig. 28). Wakemap Mound, Columbia Valley, Oregon. Idaho State University Museum, Pocatello. Photograph courtesy of B. Robert Butler. Cf. p. 81.*

Europeans. For this view two main arguments have been advanced: (1) the carving of these enormous pieces is thought to have been possible only with the aid of iron tools, and (2) the earliest travellers fail to mention totem poles. It is certain that Cook neither illustrates nor mentions a single totem pole from his voyage to the Northwest Coast, or rather he speaks only of the carved poles within the houses, which resemble the totem poles in appearance and function. The early presence of these last pieces contradicts the first argument about technical means. Moreover, one has to bear in mind that Cook did not touch the homelands of the Kwakiutl, Haida and Tsimshian, where the totem poles are found. The first illustration of a totem pole, however, dates from 1791—only shortly after Cook's voyage. Finally, since all the objects brought back by the early travellers show the same general stylistic qualities of nineteenth-century pieces, it is hardly likely that the totem pole was first created during the last century.

The illustration of legends or parts of legends was not confined to totem poles, but appeared also on painted house walls and elsewhere. A type of rattle, often called a raven rattle, may present a whole incident derived from the popular raven legend. Such scenes show how the raven carried the possessor of the halibut hook on his back. In a general sense the raven—particularly his characteristic feature, the beak—is closely connected with the realm of legend, for the ball in his beak represents the sun or the light of day, which he stole for the world's benefit. Legendary representations have been continued into quite recent times, having found their most famous expression in the argillite figure of the 'Bear Mother' carved by the Haida artist Tsagay about 1883. This popular motif presents a facet of the bear clan's legendary origin: the story of the woman Skoaoga, who married or was carried off by the lord of the bears. The child of this union was half man, half bear. It is interesting to note how differently artists conceived this blend. For example, Tsagay emphasized human features, but the child had sharp bear's teeth and the artist shows the pain Skoaoga endured when she nursed it. No doubt there is a good deal of European influence in figures of this kind, but at the same time they retained

Legends

PLATE P. 65

many stylistic qualities of the old Northwest Coast art. The dynamism and expressiveness of these works make them true sculptures in the western sense.

Argillite On the whole the use of argillite (often mistermed slate) is due to European influence. The Haida, from whose territory the argillite was obtained, were the only group to work it artistically; before contact with the Europeans, however, they used it only to make small amulets. Even later when the material became more popular, argillite was not carved for the domestic market, but only for export. The form and often the ornament of the export pieces was modified to
FIG. 27 stimulate demand. This was especially true of plates, where the carving technique of the early examples followed the scrimshaw work of the sailors of European and American ships. The ornament of these early pieces frequently recalls the decoration of European, especially Russian folk art, and must have had its source there. Later Indian argillite carvers developed a style more in harmony with
Human figures Northwest Coast art as a whole. Apart from round plates, the main objects were pipes (rarely usable), models of totem poles and free-standing figures.

Up to this point we have been mainly discussing the figures of animals with their carefully regulated conventions. Yet man too was important in the representational art of the Northwest Coast and was scarcely less often used as a model.

But while rules and conventions gave the animal figures a severe and often static appearance, no such restrictions applied to human figures. Consequently the body can be much more supple and lively, the face more expressive. Freedom of conception often favoured a portrait-like realism, as witness the masks and the so-called potlatch figures (big wooden figures placed on the roofs of houses to commemorate noteworthy potlatch feasts). Apparently these figures and faces permitted free artistic inspiration untrammelled by traditional prototypes. The only generally accepted convention—that women be shown with a lip peg—was no hindrance to the artist. Apart from the fact that human figures, in contrast to the stiffness and abstraction of the animals, appear to be full of life, it is hard to make generalizations about them. Tsagay's Bear Mother shows this vitality, for its movement

FIG. 31 – *Stone figure in the typical style of the late period of the middle Columbia. Found at The Dalles, Oregon. Photograph courtesy of Emory M. Strong. Cf. p. 81.*

and dynamism can only partly be ascribed to European influence. The boundary between animal and human figures is not a precise one; as we have seen, artists could apply animal features to a basically human form, thus indicating that its significance is supposed to be that of a creature or of a Lord of Animals.

Carving and painting make up a large part of Northwest Coast art. But they are not the only techniques cultivated and two other crafts should be mentioned: weaving and basketry. The two are closely connected, for—as mentioned at the outset of this section—weaving, which uses a 'loom' with a single warp beam, really amounts to an extension of basketry. Cedar bast was preferred for the warp, mountain-goat wool (in the north) and dog hair (in the south) for the woof. The main products of these 'looms' were blankets; the members of the Chilkat branch of the Tlingit Indians wove the best known and most interesting of these. Chilkat blankets are pentagonal with straight edges at the top and sides and a triangular projection at the bottom. The sides and the lower flap are often fringed. The hues used in the old days were the natural colour of wool, yellow, blue and black; European colours, notably green, were only introduced quite recently. The patterns of the Chilkat blankets, like those of the shirt-like garments made in the same style, were extraordinarily complicated. This is probably why they were copied from patterns rather than woven spontaneously or from memory.

Chilkat textiles

PLATE P. 74

Although the making of blankets was women's work, the patterns were designed on wooden slabs by men. This explains the connexion between textile patterns and those of carving and painting, though they may seem unrelated at first sight. First examination often discloses a bewildering wealth of faces, eyes and other motifs, which appear to have been distributed helter-skelter. The student of these patterns must possess a vast knowledge of all the conventions and submit to a long period of study—perhaps longer than anywhere else in American Indian culture. Even so the result is not fully satisfactory, for field work has shown how the inhabitants of the Northwest Coast can disagree in their explanation of the same blanket. Some scholars have suggested that the patterns are deliberately ambiguous so as to permit successive owners to interpret them in personal terms. But it is more likely that (as with totem poles) the pattern was only fully intelligible to the designer of the pattern and to the first owner.

It has been noted above that the decoration of Chilkat blankets is closely linked with that of painting and carving. This is due to the application of the same principles to different media, and thus the

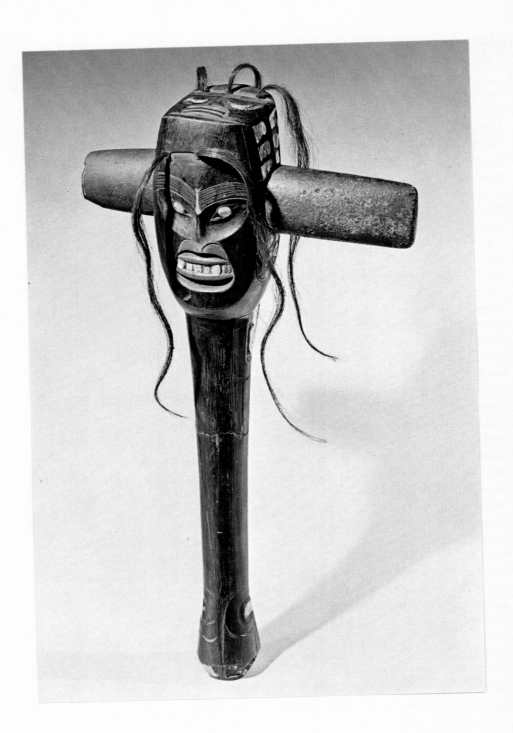

characteristics described above for animals are found here too. There is the same method of splitting an animal from the back, making a whole from two side views. The *horror vacui* principle is very important and X-ray views and eye joints are common. The combined effect of all these factors makes the basic pattern hard to recognize. Most of the faces that appear are not in fact the animal's face but only fill out the body, the ear or some other part. Only two of the eyes can be the real ones, the others being joints—though this is not certain in every case. Empty spaces are covered with filler items, each of FIG. 22 which has its name and meaning, but they are normally not employed with this significance. Of course the blankets have certain basic decorative schemes with the aid of which one can discern faces and other parts of the body, although these do not always tally and may have become unrecognizable through an excess of fillers. In many cases a central figure is present, spread out frontally, while a line (which may be omitted) divides it from two flanking figures shown in side view. Through acquaintance with these divisions and the general conventions it is sometimes possible to solve the riddle of the ornament and to hazard an interpretation. But the validity of such an interpretation is often doubtful.

Unlike the Chilkat blankets, the blankets of other groups and tribes are more simply worked and the patterns are more closely comparable with those of baskets. These baskets, which are mostly straight-sided and sometimes provided with a cover, were woven by women out of cedar roots. They are often watertight. Their decoration does not resemble that of the Northwest Coast examples discussed previously. It consists of several horizontal bands filled with repeating geometric patterns. Since the individual motifs often have names—such as bear track, geese in flight, lightning and raven's tail, to name but a few—one might conclude that they evolved out of the main body of Northwest Coast design. But this custom is fully in accord with the habit of giving names to basketry patterns found among other primitive peoples and cannot be taken as evidence for a single ornamental repertory in this region. Rather we must assume two separate repertories of ornament that may be ascribed to men and women respectively, each sex adhering to an ornamental idiom of its own.

Weaving and basketry

'Slave killer'. Painted wood with stone blades, abalone-shell inlay and hair. The interpretation of the face is uncertain, but it may be a strongly humanized bear. Kwakiutl, Alert Bay, British Columbia. *Height of handle 49.5 cm. Brooklyn Museum, Brooklyn, N. Y. Cf. p. 70.*

Blanket of cedar bast and wild-goat hair in the Chilkat style. The interpretation of the complicated style is difficult and can only be satisfactorily done with the maker's help. The faces on the blanket have nothing to do with the pattern, but represent filling in accordance with the *horror vacui* principle. The numerous eyes are mostly joints; only the two large forms right and left of the centre can be described for certain as eyes. Beneath them to one side are teeth and above are the ears. The two big horizontal fins beside the ears may refer to a killer whale or a composite creature. Chilkat sub-group of the Tlingit. *Width 1.70 m. Museum für Völkerkunde, Hamburg. Cf. pp. 71, 75.*

Up to this point we have treated the art of the Northwest Coast as a unit. For most general principles this is valid, but one might anticipate, because of the region's vast extent, some differences between the groups and linguistic units. (In the strict sense the concept of the tribe is not applicable to this region.) We must now give some attention to these differences.

Our discussion of social conditions revealed that clans were particularly important in the Northern group. Consequently the demand for objects decorated with clan insignia was much greater here than in other areas. This may also explain why totem poles, which attained their highest glory in the work of the Tsimshian and the Haida, developed here. In addition to their gigantic totem poles the Haida are noted for large-scale sculptures. Moreover, as we have seen, they were the only people to produce argillite carvings in the nineteenth century. Especially characteristic of the Tlingit—apart from very naturalistic carvings—are finely woven baskets with geometrical patterns. The Chilkat people excelled in making the clothing and blankets bearing their name.

Northern group

PLATE P. 65
FIG. 27

PLATE P. 74
FIG. 22

The conditions of the Wakash group were different: secret societies rather than clans played the essential role. Thus the art requirements are not the same, though many items remained. For example, legends of the origins of the clans in the north were told among the Wakash group in slightly altered form as the origin of their secret societies. The importance of the secret societies and dances accounts for the leading role of masks, which are characteristically dramatic and naturalistic. This is especially true of the masks of the Kwakiutl and of the Bella Coola, who were strongly influenced by the Kwakiutl in their social forms and art. Stimulated by the northern example, both these units erected totem poles. Movable objects, a speciality of this group, include hinged masks showing an animal outside and a man inside so that the dancer could change roles during the performance. During ceremonies figures with movable limbs could be manipulated by cords that were unseen in the flickering light of the fire. The third unit of this group, the Nootka, retained many older features, as we have seen. The very special style they created emerges most clearly in the wolf masks, which are angular and geometric with flat surfaces

Wakash group

PLATE P. 56

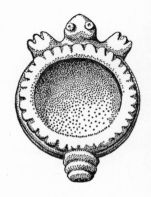

FIG. 32 – *Stone mortar in the form of a tortoise. Late Period. Found at The Dalles, Oregon. Photograph courtesy of the owner, Emory M. Strong. Cf. p. 81.*

Bowl made of horn of bighorn sheep. The excised decoration faithfully reflects the geometric tendency of the Coast Salish-Chinook group, which distinguishes their work from other carvings of Northwest Coast Indians. Chinook. *Diameter 20 cm. Royal Albert Memorial Museum, Exeter, England. Cf. p. 79.*

FIG. 33 – *Stone mortar in the form of an owl. Late Period. Found at Five Miles Locks, Long Narrows, Columbia River, Oregon. Krussow Collection. Photograph courtesy of Emory M. Strong. Cf. p. 81.*

and much painting. They also made more naturalistic masks, which were often quite large. Painting was especially favoured by the Nootka, who used it in many contexts. And they created a unique sword-like club from whale bone, which was widely traded along the coast and in the interior; its grip bore the stylized head of a thunder bird, which was partly inlaid with abalone. The form and appearance of these clubs suggest that they are fairly old, and in fact they are found in pre-European archaeological contexts.

PLATE P. 61

Taken as a whole, the Northern and Wakash groups make up the central part of Northwest Coast art. Although differences exist, boundaries are fluid and the same basic principles are everywhere employed. This continuity is broken when we shift our attention southwards to the Coast Salish-Chinook group. Only the geometrical basket decoration persists with slight variations, reaching a new high point of quality for the Northwest Coast. Sculptures and carvings, however, are quite angular, almost geometric. Despite the fact that some principles, such as the X-ray view, were retained, these recall only slightly the art of the Northern and Wakash groups. The X-ray principle appears, for example, in the rendering of ribs in figures carved by the Salish on the Thompson River. Otherwise these figures with their stiffness and highly geometrical faces have no connexion with the vital human figures found farther north. Moreover, their function is different: the figures, which are set up around the shaman's house during ceremonies, represent spirits who collaborate with him. Belief in spirits is the outstanding characteristic of this group, possibly because neither clans nor secret societies were well enough developed to displace it. As a result there was no occasion to produce masks, crests and the like. The legends, which in the north often stimulated artistic activity, simply explained the origin of the basic unit, the village. These legends were enacted in dances and song, the two main cultural manifestations of this group. Masks, for example, are only found among the Cowichan on the northern fringe of this group. They represent without doubt an influence from the Kwakiutl, but only the ideas, not the shapes were transmitted. These are highly geometrical and accord well with the Salish style already mentioned. Geometric designs were also extensively used by the Chinook living at the mouth of the

Coast Salish-Chinook group

FIG. 28

FIG. 29

Columbia River, as attested by their characteristic bowls made from wood or the horn of bighorn sheep.

PLATE P. 76

Finally, the fourth and southernmost of the Northwest culture complexes, the north-west California group, provides a link with the neighbouring Californian tribes. Although they adopted certain traits of the Northwest Coast Indians, the north-west Californian Indians were influenced in so many ways, especially in material culture and art, by their southern neighbours that they are best discussed in connexion with California proper.

At this point, however, we must turn to yet another region which had close links with the Northwest Coast—especially in art. This is the interior Plateau region, drained by the Fraser and the Columbia Rivers which flow into the ocean in the southern part of the Northwest Coast. These rivers provided channels of contact which in historical times furthered active trade between the coast and the interior. Thus the wealth of the Chinook, who created the competitive potlatch, depended primarily on the trade-routes following the course of the Columbia; because of their location at the mouth of this river the Chinook played an important part as middlemen. It is possible and indeed quite likely that these arrangements already existed in pre-European times. This assumption is strengthened by the fact that a large part of the Plateau was settled by tribes who also belonged to the Salish linguistic family and who are known collectively as the Inland Salish. All factors known up to date combine to indicate that every member of this linguistic group originally lived in the interior, though some of them subsequently migrated to the coast. Migration in the opposite direction seems unlikely.

Archaeology of the Middle Columbia

In the field of archaeology we are much better informed about the Plateau region (the middle Columbia in particular) than about the Northwest Coast. The series, known primarily from The Dalles where it was obtained under the River Basin Program, reflects a development whose oldest manifestations go back to about 6000 B.C. The Old Cordilleran tradition, which was diffused in the Plateau region and elsewhere, as well as the following Desert tradition of the Proto-Archaic

Pliable carrying-bag in twined technique. The human and animal figures, which have acquired a skeleton-like appearance due to application of the X-ray principle, represent a direct continuation of pre-European art (cf. Fig. 28). Wasco. *Height about 25 cm. Denver Art Museum, Colo. Cf. p. 82.*

FIG. 34 – *Decorated smoking tube in stone. Late Period of the middle Columbia. Photograph courtesy of Emory M. Strong. Cf. p. 81.*

period, which begins about 6000 B.C., have already been mentioned in the first chapter of this book. For the Plateau region and for the Great Basin to the south these two traditions form a basis that persisted unchanged for a long time. But it seems that relatively early a phase of specialization set in on the Columbia, its chief distinguishing feature being the economic advantages of fishing in the river. Precisely when this specialization began is still disputed, but it was certainly under way at the beginning of our era and had spread far over the Plateau, which grew more and more independent of its southern allegiance. At this time stone sculpture was already widespread and relatively well developed.

The Wakemap series coming after A.D. 500 signalled the culmination of this art. As in historical times, it can be assumed that many tribes and groups gathered above The Dalles on the Long Narrows of the Columbia when the 'run' of the salmon began, for this stretch was one of the best fishing grounds known. To accommodate the thousands of people who came to fish temporary settlements were put up here but the permanent inhabitants were never more than a few hundred in number. At the same time a lively barter trade grew up; ideas as well as goods were exchanged. One should not underrate the importance of these originally trading encounters for the diffusion of objects, ideas, prototypes and styles. In their extended seasonal migrations these semi-nomadic tribes came into contact with the most diverse cultures, borrowing objects from them and passing them on later to others in the course of similar gatherings. Thus things from one tribe reached another without any direct contact between the two. It is certain that traders and groups from the coast also flocked to these gatherings on the Long Narrows, for many cultural traits show a close link with the Northwest Coast. To take one example, these Indians, like the Coast Salish, lived in rectangular houses with a wooden frame covered with mats. Moreover, the custom of cremating the dead was common to the two groups.

We know their art as a result of excavations in an area now covered by the artificial lake created by The Dalles Dam. By a lucky chance along the middle Columbia there have been preserved not only stone objects, but also pieces of bone and horn which give us considerable

insight into the artistic achievement of the region. In art as in the culture as a whole two phases must be distinguished; the earlier lasted from A.D. 900 to 1400, the later from 1400 to 1800, when the Europeans came. In the earlier period both commodities, such as stone mortars with incised geometrical patterns, and ornaments were developed. Noteworthy among the latter are pectorals in fish form, which characteristically show the X-ray view known from the Northwest Coast. This principle may be further observed in bone objects in human form, where it is sometimes confined to the indication of ribs alone. The similarity to the wooden figures of the Coast Salish of the Thompson River is unmistakable.

After A.D. 1400 the influence of the Northwest Coast increased. Big stone figures made their first appearance in a very typical and striking style. Note the projecting eyes, the mouth in half-moon form, the rich ornament of the hair and ears, and the suggestion of ribs and vertebrae. The flat treatment of the faces of these figures recalls the wood figures of the coast. Among animal figures the popular owls and beavers embellish small stone mortars used for grinding pigment. Unlike the more static art works of the Northwest Coast, animals carved on   FIG. 33
the middle Columbia often appear in action—the owls, for example, have outstretched wings as if preparing for flight. Stone was a popular medium; apart from the above-mentioned objects, pestles, mallets, weights for spear-throwers and the characteristic funnel-shaped smoking tubes were made from this material. These objects were   FIG. 34
frequently decorated with incised lines. Carvings in bone and horn were generally more highly developed than in the earlier period; a definite shift in style had taken place. These carvings, unlike the earlier almost geometrically simple pieces, appear overloaded and scholars have adduced the influence of the *horror vacui* principle of the   FIG. 35
Northwest Coast to account for this. A horn carving from the Over site in the Spedis Valley near the Long Narrows proves that influence from this district was very important. This piece combines stylistic   FIG. 36
elements from three areas. The crescent mouth and the incised ribs are typical of the middle Columbia Valley, the general area of discovery. The circles containing a point and the triangle originate in Plateau art. Finally, the eye joints are known to us from the Northwest

Coast. Probably no object from this district shows so clearly how styles interpenetrated and fused in this region.

It is quite possible that a portion of the objects attributed to a later period were made here by the Wasco, a Chinook-speaking tribe on the south side of the Long Narrows, or by the related Wishram on the opposite (Washington State) side. This is suggested by the following facts: these Indians were found living in these areas by the first explorers; they had the same way of life that is documented by archaeological finds; many of their artistic products were also the same.

PLATE P. 78 Thus the decorative patterns of their cylindrical pouches, woven according to a special technique, represent the continuation of the older art. The human figures on them, produced by the Wasco in the twentieth century, show the typical rib representation with the X-ray view that had for so long been a feature of art in this district.

In historical times the other Plateau tribes, which belong to the Salish and Shahaptian linguistic families, for the most part adopted the horse and with it many traits of the Great Plains culture, with which they are more appropriately discussed.

FIG. 36 – *Richly carved horn object of the Late Period combining style elements of the Northwest Coast, the Plateau region and the middle Columbia. Found at Over site, Spedis Valley, Oregon. Idaho State University Museum, Pocatello. Photograph courtesy of B. Robert Butler. Cf. p. 81.*

V. CALIFORNIA

As an archaeological and ethnological unit California corresponds *Geography* in area to that of the present-day American state—that is to say, it extends from the Sierra Nevada Mountains and the Colorado River in the east to the Pacific Ocean in the west. The northern and central parts can be reached from the east only by a few mountain passes, while southern California is accessible from the Nevada and Arizona deserts, as well as from Mexico. Moreover, the southern coastal plain is both wider and drier than its northern counterpart. With its narrow, deep valleys and thick pine forests the north contrasts with the gentler and broader valleys of the centre and south, which favour oak forests. The middle part of the state takes on a special character owing to the presence of a wide intramontane valley watered by the Sacramento and San Joaquin Rivers.

Despite these environmental contrasts California underwent a relatively uniform cultural development, which was only modified in limited areas by small groups of outsiders. The component units, which stemmed from almost all the great North American linguistic families, created the mosaic of numerous small tribes known from historical times. But they generally seem to have been absorbed quite rapidly into the 'Californian basic culture', which rested on the same economic foundations from about 5000 B.C. Here and there the emphasis varied in response to local conditions, but the basic tendencies always persisted or reasserted themselves anew.

In Californian archaeology three provinces—south, centre and north— **ARCHAEOLOGY** can be distinguished, which in turn can be subdivided into distinct

FIG. 37 – *Soapstone swordfish with eyes inlaid in shell. Gabrielino. After Douglas and D'Harnoncourt, 1941. Cf. p. 87.*

areas from west to east, as one proceeds inland from the coast. Although each of these subgroups has its archaeological justification and shows special features, we shall not enter into these in detail, for this would complicate the picture unnecessarily. In any case few art objects have come to light from the early cultures of this area and a generalizing treatment seems more appropriate.

Generally Californian archaeology is divided into three main periods, each of which falls into several phases which do not interest us here. The Early Period, beginning about 5000 B.C., shows flat milling stones with stone grinders, so that in southern California one speaks of the 'Milling Stone Horizon'. The repertory of this horizon is a simple one, pointing to a hunting and collecting economy in which products from the sea had a certain importance. Offshoots of this horizon are found as far as northern California, though in changed form.

In the Middle Period from 2000 B.C. onwards mortars and pestles appeared in increasing numbers. The mortars were of stone, wood or else of stone with a basketry hopper. Milling stones also continued to be made, though they were less common. This may indicate that the acorn economy (see below) was well under way, dominating economic life. This assumption is also supported by the growth of villages in this period, a development that would have required an assured economic base. Certain changes are also indicated by a shift from primary burials in extended position to tightly flexed ones. Although in many respects uniformity persists throughout the California cultural area, one finds in central California, especially in the Sacramento and San Joaquin Valleys and along the coast south of San Francisco, certain harbingers of the following period. It is possible, however, that this reflects the present incomplete state of our archaeological knowledge. Apart from the additional objects woven in twining technique, the repertory of the central area includes a new line of basketry in coiling technique. Shells and abalone were used for ornament and flat pierced disks may possibly have served as money. Bone was popular for many types of objects. In addition to the burial types mentioned for the region as a whole, cremation was practised in some instances.

In the succeeding Late Period, which began between A.D. 300 and A.D. 500, links with the later tribes can often be discerned fairly easily. During this period objects that had first made their appearance in central California spread over the whole region. Cremation of the dead and the use of curved fish hooks made of shell were general. Other new features of this culture, for example the use of asphalt and soapstone, were found notably in southern and adjacent parts of central California. Crude pots were also made at this time. In southern California these and the soapstone vessels were mutually exclusive. In northern California, which only appears clearly on the archaeological horizon toward the end of the Late Period, changes occurred of which the significance has not yet been clarified. Influences from the North may have begun much earlier than this late date. This is shown, for instance, by the animal-like 'slave killers' made of stone, which reveal certain similarities with corresponding pieces of the Northwest Coast.

As has been pointed out above, in historical times California was inhabited by many small tribes of the most varied language affiliations. Nonetheless, a 'Californian basic culture' was present, which despite some variations characterized all the tribes. They did not practise agriculture. The maize-growing Indians of the lower Colorado River, which forms the boundary between California and Arizona,

Soapstone smoking tube with shell beads inlaid in asphalt. This particularly fine piece displays a lizard in flat relief. Santa Barbara County, Calif. Chumash (?). *Length 42.5 cm. Museum of the American Indian, Heye Foundation, New York, N. Y. Cf. p. 87.*

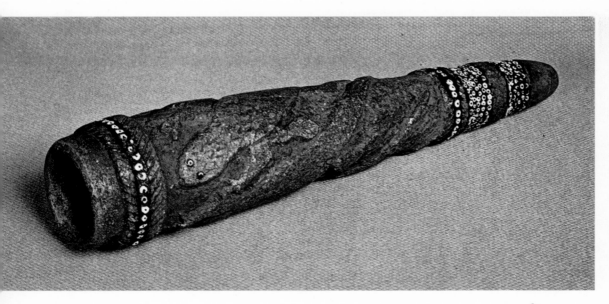

belong to the Southwest region, from which they derived their cultural stimulus. The acorn provided the chief source of food for the Californian Indians, who extracted a debittered meal from it by a complicated process; the meal was stockpiled for the winter in large baskets. In addition they collected and prepared chestnuts, grass-seeds, roots and bulbs. Food was also obtained from the sea: here molluscs were collected, fish caught and sea mammals hunted. Hunting on land further supplemented their diet, though it was only significant for the interior tribes. The wealth of food available to gatherers makes it likely that agriculture was never attempted, for the yield of collecting was in no way inferior to that of simple agriculture and thus the Indians could settle in large villages for the winter with few worries about the food supply. This abundance explains the density of population found in California before the arrival of the Europeans; this density surpassed that of many agricultural regions. It is estimated that the California cultural bloc included about thirteen per cent of the pre-European population of North America, whereas the surface area accounted for little more than two per cent of the whole.

Apart from the common food base, other features were shared by all or most of the California tribes. These include cremation of the dead in southern and central California, shell money, advanced basketry, circular fish hooks, mortars and pestles, basketry hats in the northern and southern parts, sweat houses, a certain degree of influence by chiefs, extensive puberty rites and well defined, carefully guarded

FIG. 38 – *Basket of willow bast woven in the coil technique. The red and black 'flame pattern' set against a golden-brown ground was named 'We gather to discuss the happy life of our ancestors' by the woman who made it, Dat-so-la-lee. The piece is one of the finest examples of Washo basketry. After Dockstader, 1962. Cf. p. 90.*

FIG. 39 – *Detail from a round woven tray for a dice game. The second strip from the edge is called 'rattlesnake pattern'. Yokut, Tulare style. After Merwin, 1918. Cf. p. 90.*

tribal territories. Among the negative traits which many units had in common, besides the absence of agriculture, the lack of masks may be mentioned.

On this basis a number of cultures were developed, of which several will be mentioned here, mainly on account of their art products. In this connexion both regional and tribal differences may be observed. In southern California particular interest attaches to the Shoshonean *Southern California* Gabrielino, their kin in the vicinity of present-day Los Angeles, and the Chumash in the Santa Barbara district who belong to the Hoka family. The latter tribe lived on the coast and on the Channel Islands, building domed huts of branches. These Chumash were oriented towards the ocean, where the hunting of sea mammals played a particularly important role. It is disputed, however, whether this hunting took place on the high seas. In any case the Chumash had sea-going boats made of planks sewn together with sinews and caulked with asphalt, holding up to thirty persons, which would have made such hunting possible. Important among the products of their material culture are soapstone vessels, which are sometimes decorated with incised lines and inlaid with shell beads set in asphalt. These shell beads also served as money. Soapstone was further used for smoking PLATE P. 85 tubes similarly inlaid in shell, which sometimes display animals in low relief. Finally, there are figures in soapstone, including killer whales, FIG. 37 sailfish and swordfish, which are modelled in the full round with an extraordinary realism: they rank among the most naturalistic animal

87

figures known from North America. Since all these objects come from excavations their function is unclear. It can be assumed, however, that they served in rituals for fishing and sea-mammal hunting.

Another manifestation of art is found among the Luiseño and Cupeño Indians. At the end of the puberty rites the young girls race to specified places where they paint stones with zigzag lines and rows of lozenges in red ochre. Both designs are said to represent rattlesnakes. In another connexion we have already mentioned the complicated rock drawings and paintings of the Santa Barbara district. Whether these should be linked to the Chumash who inhabited the district in historical times remains uncertain, primarily because the dating cannot be ascertained with any precision. While paintings on open rock faces have a short lifetime, this criterion is obviously not applicable to cave paintings such as the Santa Barbara ones.

As has already been noted, basketry reached a high state of perfection in California, becoming the most important art form of the area. And in fact nowhere else in America was basketry practised with greater variety and technical finish. Unfortunately only a few examples have survived from earlier times. The mass of baskets available for study come from the 'Renaissance' of the art in the twentieth century. Comparison has shown, however, that technique, patterns and execution correspond quite closely to those of earlier specimens. Because of the mass of tribes, almost every one of which has its own distinctive style and forms, its own preferences in pattern and colour, it is impossible to give an exhaustive survey of the varied manifestations of this art. We must restrict ourselves to singling out a few general features of specific districts and to describing the products of especially important and artistically noteworthy tribes.

In southern California baskets were uniformly coiled, that is, a foundation made of coarse material, used either in one or several strands, was interwoven with bast or straw of various plants. The needles required for this work were usually made of bone: where the baskets have disappeared the survival of these needles proves the earlier existence of the technique. Especially noteworthy are the plaited

Basket woven in coiling technique and lined externally with feathers. A row of shell disks runs round the rim and shell disks also function as pendants, to which are attached figural and geometrically cut abalone-shell pieces. This richly decorated basket is supposed to be a copy of one in which, according to a myth, the sun was brought from another world. Yuki. *Diameter of the basket 33 cm; total height including handle and pendants 66 cm. U. S. National Museum, Washington, D. C. Cf. p. 92.*

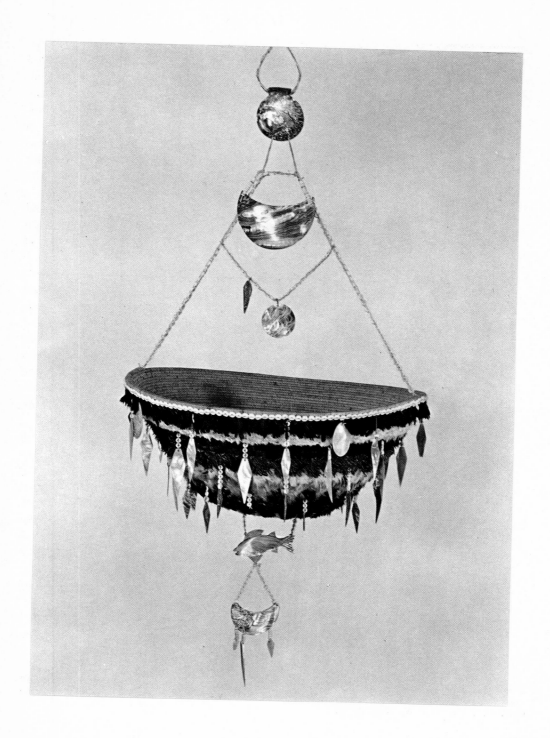

objects of the Mission Indians (Gabrielino, Luiseño and related tribes). The patterns in cream and black set off against a brown-speckled background proceed radially from the centre of the baskets—which are often rather flat—to the edge. The frequent curved lines and the occasional plant decoration reflect the influence of Spanish missionaries. The small tribes of the interior of southern California, such as the Chemehuevi and Panamint, originally favoured a black geometrical pattern on a whitish ground; later, under European influence, other colours were added. The baskets of these tribes commonly take the bottle form.

Washo
Many of the central California groups have developed a very special style for the decoration of their baskets and thereby gained a certain renown. Among these are the Hoka-speaking Washo on the edge of the Sierra Nevada range, whose typically spherical baskets are coiled. The background colours range from white to cream and the patterns appear in red and black. The Washo ornaments can be recognized quite easily, being distinguished from the others by the fact that they are composed of elongated triangles, which are sometimes called 'flames', because they point upwards. Around the turn of the century a special renown was achieved by the Washo woman weaver Dat-so-la-lee, who named her baskets according to the pattern used. But in the
FIG. 38
example illustrated here, which is called 'we gather to discuss the happy life of our ancestors', the title does not seem to elucidate the pattern.

Tulare
An entirely different style is found in the southern part of the San Joaquin Valley. The main exponents of this style were the Penutian-speaking Yokut and other tribes living in Tulare County, so that it
FIG. 39
is sometimes referred to as the Tulare style. The round and oval bowls and the flat plates that served as a base for dice games were coiled. The black and red decoration is set off by a bright ground. Characteristic are the bands of red lozenges or triangles, which are explained as rattlesnakes; these bands may be arranged either horizontally or vertically on the basket surface.

Another typical pattern consists of stylized human figures with joined hands.

Woman's apron made of shells, seeds and coloured beads. The old geometric patterns persist despite the use of modern materials. Tolowa. *Length 74 cm.; width 53 cm. Museum of the American Indian, Heye Foundation, New York, N. Y. Cf. p. 94.*

Pomo   Other tribes of the central valley, such as the Maidu, were strongly influenced by the Pomo, who lived on the coast. The latter were virtuoso basketmakers. Their products, both coiled and twined, evoked the admiration of the first explorers, who have left accounts of

FIG. 41   them. Carrying baskets were bell- or funnel-shaped; other types were globular, hemispherical and, less commonly, funnel-shaped. The geometrical, often diagonally developed patterns were executed in red and black against a brownish-to-cream ground. The lively patterns, the fine, precise weaving procedures and the size (ranging from thumbnail miniatures to pieces the height of a man) assured the fame of this

PLATE P. 89   basketry. The Pomo and their neighbours, among whom the Yuki are the most important, were particularly well known for the special added decoration of their so-called 'gift baskets', a name applied to them by the Americans because these baskets were used as gifts on certain occasions for example, at weddings. The finest of these were richly bedecked with black, yellow, red, orange and green feathers, which often formed a four-armed whorl with its centre at the base. Moreover, the edge was decorated with shell disks and hangings—shells and abalone carvings representing figures.

Ornaments of the commoner 'gift baskets' were limited to tufts of feathers and or shell disks. European and American influence is evident in the use of coloured glass beads, which may cover the whole basket. The Pomo applied feathers to other objects as well, such as shoulder bands and hair- and ear-pieces. In this technique they achieved a mastery that was unique in North America and which may be compared only with the famed products of the high cultures of Peru and Mexico.

North-west California   As has already been indicate, the culture of the north-west Californian tribes, the Hupa, Karok, Yurok, Tolowa and their neighbours, was a mixture of Californian culture elements with others from the North-west Coast. This intermediate position can already be noted in the economic life of these tribes. Acorn meal and deer hunting, two features typical of California, played an important role. But fishing also contributed a great deal to the food supply and in this many

Painted stone mortar. The pattern in red and greenish white reflects the geometric style also found in pottery that is typical of the Anasazi tradition. Great Pueblo period, Anasazi tradition. Found at Pueblo Bonito, N. M. *Height 22.6 cm. Museum of the American Indian, Heye Foundation, New York, N. Y. Cf. p. 109.*

VI. THE SOUTHWEST

Geography The Southwest, which comprises most of the present states of Arizona, New Mexico, Utah and Colorado, lies mainly in the vast arid zone that we have already encountered in southern California. Ecologically, the Southwest does not form a homogeneous whole, but is divided into many small units tending to follow one another without transition. In general three geographical zones can be distinguished as we move from north to south. The northern zone presents a plateau area broken by deep canyons, among which the Grand Canyon is world famous. The mesas (flat-topped rocky hills with steeply sloping sides), which rise in the areas between the canyons, had pine and juniper forests; the canyons and the wider valleys had brush vegetation. The water table of the area lies many feet below the ground. Winter rain and occasional cloudbursts in summer, which briefly flood the otherwise dry valleys with sheets of water, were and still are important features of the region. Better watered is the mountainous zone to the south, with peaks reaching a height of 13,000 feet. This zone is broken up too, but the valleys are gentler and have broader flood-plains along the rivers. Pine forests flourish here. Least favoured by nature is the southernmost zone which reaches as far as Mexico; it can be described as desert or semi-desert. Cactus, yucca and other arid zone plants provide the characteristic vegetation.

In these difficult circumstances one might expect that only a few isolated nomadic groups would appear, as was the case in the environmentally somewhat similar Great Basin lying to the north. But in the Southwest agriculture was firmly established well before the coming of the Europeans. With their specialized irrigation and dry farming methods, these Indians reached heights unknown elsewhere in North America. As far as we can determine, the operative stimulus came from the Mexican high culture area to the south via a culture corridor beginning in Durango in the eastern foothills of the Sierra Madre Occidental. Over this 'highway', whose true importance has only recently been recognized, maize or Indian corn reached the Southwest about 2500 B.C., though initially it did not produce any great changes in the existing Cochise culture (a specialized subgroup in the Desert tradition). The Indians of the Cochise culture were semi-nomadic collectors who, like later historical groups of the Great Basin, were accustomed to move about according to the seasons and possibly to sow certain native wild plants. For them maize was merely a supplementary food source with no far-reaching effects. The appearance of beans and pumpkins in the region about 1000 B.C. seems to have been equally ineffective in changing the way of life. Thus a 'Neolithic agricultural revolution', which is often assumed to have taken place, occurred here—if at all—only much later. For only the shift at the beginning of the Christian era can be regarded in this way. At this time, together with new varieties of maize (perhaps imported from Mexico) permanent settlements appeared, which already indicate the three great traditions of the Southwest.

Archaeologically, the Southwest is the best known region in North America. Not only do the sequences with ascertained dates follow one another without a gap thanks to the tree-ring chronology, but because of the climate many objects of perishable material have been preserved which give us a more complete picture than is the case with other North American archaeological cultures. Thus it happens that a finely nuanced classification has been built up, dividing the major cultures into branches, periods and phases, and making the Southwest a testing ground and point of departure for the archaeology of the American continent. We cannot enter into the details of classification, for they would fill the whole book. The discussion will be restricted to the main lines of development of the three great cultural traditions and a few smaller units that are less well known. In the survey that follows three artistic aspects will be reserved for collective treatment later: architecture, painting and pottery.

About 300 B.C. the first stage of the Mogollon culture is to be found in the upper Gila valley and on the Mimbres in New Mexico; this developed from the San Pedro stage of the Cochise culture. The cultivation of maize, beans and pumpkins seems to have been already known, for in contrast to the Cochise culture the Indians lived in villages of irregularly distributed pit houses, which included semi-subterranean 'ceremonial houses'. Together with baskets and bone tools, which closely resemble those of the preceding phase, unpainted red pottery appears at this time. Bows and arrows replace the spears and

Mogollon

FIG. 42 – *Jet pendant with turquoise inlay in the shape of a frog. Regressive Pueblo stage, Anasazi tradition. Found at Pueblo Bonito, Room 38. After Pepper, 1920. Cf. p. 109.*

97

throwers previously dominant. Other stone objects include grinding stones of different types with the appropriate handstones, as well as mortars, pestles, mallets, crude tools for scraping and cutting and rudimentary pipes (smoking tubes). The dead were buried in a flexed position.

Mogollon I lasted until about A.D. 400. The remaining four stages are not very different: they can only be distinguished through changes in ceramics, which were decorated from the second stage onwards. During these stages the Mogollon tradition attained its greatest geographical extent, including southern New Mexico, south-eastern Arizona and a large portion of the border lands of northern Mexico. With the fifth stage, however, considerable changes take place (about A.D. 1000), which came not from the tradition itself, but through foreign infiltration from the Anasazi culture lying to the north. In addition to radical changes in ceramics, houses are now built above ground and kivas are constructed. Towards 1150 the Mogollon tradition was practically obliterated and incorporated into the Anasazi tradition. Geographical factors may account for this development. Initially the mountain zone in which these Indians lived resembled the slopes of the Mexican Sierra Madre Occidental and thus favoured the introduction of maize and the methods that had been developed for its cultivation. Later, however, it hindered larger accumulations of population by isolating the inhabitants in small valleys. This led to cultural backwardness vis-à-vis their neighbours, who were now actively acquiring ideas and techniques from the Meso-American high cultures.

Hohokam About the beginning of our era and not much later than Mogollon the first (Pioneer) stage of the Hohokam tradition developed from the San Pedro stage. The beginnings of the Pioneer stage may be identified in the territory of the lower Gila. Apparently because it had the same basis and experienced the same influences, this stage closely resembles the first Mogollon stage. In the Pioneer stage agriculture was practised in flood areas and villages consisted of unaligned pit houses. Identifiable ceremonial buildings were missing. Besides unpainted and monochrome pottery, bichrome ceramics and crude pottery figurines were also manufactured. The working of stone was already a specialty in this period and many tools and objects were made of it. Among these, apart from trough-like grinding stones and grooved axes of diorite, the flat palettes are particularly attractive, though their function is obscure. Local turquoise and shells imported from the Pacific coast were used to make simple jewellery. Although bone tools are less common than in the other traditions, the decorated tubes of unknown purpose deserve special mention. The dead were cremated and their ashes buried with offerings in simple pits.

The second, the Colonial stage of the Hohokam tradition, begins about A.D. 600. It lasted for some three hundred years, spreading over southern Arizona. While the Mogollon culture flourished mainly in the mountainous parts of the Southwest and only penetrated the southern desert area later, the Hohokam tradition was always present in this arid region. Although flood agriculture sufficed for the needs of the first settlements of the Poineer stage, it was clear that this method would not suffice to feed a growing population. Consequently irrigation

Small stone bowl with relief decoration. In the Southwest naturalistic motifs are a hallmark of the Hohokam tradition. Apart from men, they depict the animal world of the surrounding desert. Slightly stylized lizards, as shown here, were particularly favoured. Rincon phase, Sedentary period, Hohokam tradition. Found at Hodges site, Ariz. *Height 5 cm.; diameter 7.5 cm. Arizona State Museum, Tucson. Cf. p. 100.*

canals were dug for maize and probably for cotton, which seems to have been imported from Mexico at this time. We do not know for certain whether this new farming technique came from Mexico, but since irrigation appeared fully developed in Arizona without recognizable earlier stages, and since similar systems were in use in the Mexican state of Puebla before the beginning of our era, a southern origin is highly probable. Canals were and are community projects that presuppose a well functioning social organization. But this advance is otherwise scarcely reflected in the Colonial stage, for the villages with their pit houses differ little from those of the preceding stage. No principles of 'town planning' emerge and there are no larger buildings indicating social stratification or a strong chieftainship. The only innovation lies in the appearance of large oval ball-courts with walls of earth or sun-dried brick (adobe); this custom was another import from Mexico. Since architecture and pottery will be considered

PLATE P. 99 more fully below, no special treatment is required here. But the stone implements must be mentioned, especially mortars, palettes and vessels that were now richly decorated with reliefs. Apart from geometrical patterns on the rim of the palettes, many life-like motifs were used: snakes, birds and human figures. The same motifs recur in the decoration of pendants, rings and arm-bands made of shells. Along with cotton, ball-courts and probably irrigation, mosaic-incrusted pyrite mirrors must be added to the list of imports from Mexico. Cremation of the dead continued.

During the following two hundred years, until A.D. 1100, the Hohokam tradition was characterized by the Sedentary stage which many regard as the climax of the development. Some southern districts were abandoned during this period, but the central region along the lower Gila and the Salt River was retained and an expansion northwards into the Verde Valley was undertaken. In general there are no major cultural changes during this period as compared with the Colonial stage. Irrigation was more intensively practised; the ball-courts were smaller and oriented in a north-south instead of an east-west direction; the pit houses were sometimes surrounded by straight walls; and oc-casional adobe houses appear on the surface. The stonecutter's art declined greatly and patterns were either geometrical or heavily
FIG. 43 stylized; personal ornaments constitute the only exception. By contrast shell work reached a high point of development. The craftsmen carved pendants out of shell and assembled rings and arm-bands of the same material. It provided a foundation for mosaics made from turquoise and these were also painted in several colours. Most re-

View of a kiva at Pueblo Bonito, Chaco Canyon, N. M. Only stumps remain of the stone piers that originally supported the roof. Between them runs a continuous bench. On the far side the opening of the ventilator shaft is visible; in front of it lies the round fire-place. Great Pueblo period, Anasazi tradition. *Cf. p. 116.*

FIG. 43 – *Fragment of shell with human figure carved in flat relief. Sedentary stage, Hohokam tradition. Found at the Grewe site, Arizona. After Douglas and D'Harnoncourt, 1941. Cf. p. 100.*

markable is the fact that at this time the decoration could be etched into shells, a technique that did not appear in Europe until the sixteenth century. The slightly acid sap of a cactus fruit served as the etching medium. The few preserved remains suggest that textile weaving was highly developed. Apart from mosaic mirrors of pyrite, in some cases made locally, copper bells were imported from Mexico, marking the first appearance of metal in the Southwest. Cremation of the dead continued, though isolated burials also occur.

The Classic stage, which is placed between A.D. 100 and 1400, saw great changes in the Hohokam tradition—changes that were brought about by the intrusion of two foreign groups into the homeland of the tradition. The first of these seems to have been the Sinagua, who will be discussed below, and the second the Salado, a branch of the Anasazi tradition. They had originally lived on the Little Colorado and possibly had their ultimate source in the Mogollon tradition. About A.D. 1100 the Salado appeared in the Tonto basin on the north-eastern fringe of the Hohokam region. Then about 1300 we find their products intermingled with those of the Hohokam on the Gila and the Salt. In this period they clearly belonged to the Anasazi tradition, as will be explained below, though they also displayed particularities of their own, especially in ceramics. To all appearances no overt conflict took place; both groups of people lived side by side in the same settlements —now grown quite large—and they worked together in the maintenance and extension of the irrigation systems, which reached their peak in this phase. In addition to maize and cotton, beans and pumpkins, which were probably introduced by the Salado, were cultivated.

Even before the actual invasion of the Gila-Salt region the Hohokam people seem to have been strongly influenced by the Salado who then lived in the Tonto region, as their architecture shows: one need only mention that from this time onward houses above ground were the fashion, while the traditional pit houses gradually went out of use. Villages grew bigger and were often walled; some of them contained an artificial earthen hill with vertical retaining walls and on this platform light houses were built. But ball-courts are absent from the settlements of the Classic stage. The hitherto highly developed art of the Hohokam disappeared altogether: shell etching, the production of palettes and vessels of stone, the use of animal and human figures as ornaments, pyrite mirrors and copper bells. But the Mexican connexion was not completely severed, as the appearance of genuine inlay mosaics and snail trumpets proves. Moreover, the idea for the platform-hill mentioned above may have come from the south. For the most part, the dead were still cremated, though the Salado brought with them the custom of inhumation, which they retained.

This seemingly peaceful coexistence ended about 1400, when the Salado left the area in order to reinforce the concentration of the Anasazi tradition (see below). What became of the Hohokam inheritance is disputed, but the majority of archaeologists feel that the present-day Pima and Papago may well be descendants of this tradition who have sunk back to the cultural level of the Pioneer stage. This account of the Hohokam tradition is accepted by most archaeologists of the Southwest. But the very strong southern influence suggests another interpretation—that at the beginning of the Colonial stage the Hohokam people migrated from Mexico, creating a basically Meso-American culture in Arizona. This theory splits off the Pioneer stage and sets up a new tradition, the Ootam, which persisted in the south as the so-called Desert Hohokam branch. These very much simpler cultural forms, which were not subject to Salado influence, then formed the basis for the present-day Pima. A variation of this view connects the Pioneer stage with the as yet unmentioned Patayan and Sinagua cultures, which are linked to form the Hakataya tradition. Only further excavations can finally demonstrate which of these three theories is correct, though the first and fullest one seems inherently the most plausible.

The third main cultural tradition of the Southwest was the Anasazi *Anasazi* tradition. Because of its large buildings erected on the surface it was the first to be found and scholars long considered it the basic source of the prehistoric cultures of this region, while the other traditions were treated as offshoots. That these views have since greatly altered is apparent from what has been said about the Mogollon and Hohokam traditions. The Anasazi tradition has been variously subdivided, but the differences pertain more to nomenclature of the several phases than to substance. The two most common systems, the so-called Pecos Classification, and the Roberts Classification, will be used here.

According to the Pecos Classification the Anasazi tradition begins with the Basketmaker I stage, which constitutes a transition from the Desert tradition. But to this day no concrete evidence for this stage has come to light and there is serious doubt whether it exists at all, for the presumably later Basketmaker II (Pecos) or Basketmaker (Roberts) stage can still be interpreted as an aftermath of the Desert tradition.

The Basketmaker tradition was at home in the drainage system of the San Juan near the junction of the four American states of Utah, Colorado, Arizona and New Mexico. Its influence is particularly noticeable throughout the plateau district, notably in Utah and northern Arizona. Maize and pumpkins were certainly grown, but there is no real indication of systematic agriculture. Possibly the way of life was still semi-nomadic, for caves and hollows were used as shelter, though huts with a slightly depressed floor also appear. Likewise, resort to many wild fruits and a strong dependence on hunting, which was done with nets and slings, as well as with spears, indicates a nomadic life. Thanks to favourable circumstances of preservation we are well informed about the material culture of this stage. And in fact the study of objects of perishable materials is indispensable, for with the exception of some sun-dried plates pottery was still unknown and, apart from knives and spear points, stone was used only to make milling stones, scrapers and smoking tubes. The mass of finds consists of basketry, hence the name Basketmaker: flat basins, bowls, funnel-shaped carrying baskets and spherical containers with a narrow opening were made in the coil technique. Patterns of red or black fibre served as decoration. The baskets were often finely woven to hold liquids and to serve as cookers through the introduction of previously heated stones. Big water containers were sometimes lined with pitch. In the twining technique, which was also used, the Indians made pouches and sometimes baskets. Very important were plaited sandals. Other items of dress were scanty: cord aprons for women and sometimes capes, which were braided with cords wrapped in fur strips and intended for both sexes, are the only garments known. Personal ornaments made from seeds, feathers, beads of bone, shell and stone were abun-

General view of Pueblo Bonito, Chaco Canyon, N.M. The extremities of the crescent-shaped main block, which originally rose to the height of four storeys, are linked by a single straight row of dwellings. Some of the round kivas were dug in the semi-circular plaza, others incorporated in the building complex itself. Great Pueblo period, Anasazi tradition. *Cf. pp. 116, 119.*

FIG. 44 – *Pottery bowl in the Mimbres black-on-white style. Fifth stage of the Mogollon tradition. Found at Swarts Ruin, New Mexico. After Cosgrove, 1932. Cf. p. 127.*

dant, though not aesthetically very pleasing. The dead were buried in a flexed position in caves or under the house floor.

Only about A.D. 400 with the appearance of the Modified Basketmaker stage—Basketmaker III according to the Pecos Classification—can one speak of the beginning of sedentary life and a real assertion of the Anasazi tradition. To the original San Juan core was added the valley of the Little Colorado, much of Utah and the upper Rio Grande district in New Mexico. The improvement in the way of life has been attributed to a new variety of maize, which now appears together with beans and which was probably imported from the south. But the Mogollon tradition, with which these people were in contact, does not seem to have been the source. On the other hand, the Anasazi people took over from the Mogollon the practice of constructing pit dwellings, though their store houses were a special development. The latter were usually situated behind the dwelling houses. Another borrowing from the Mogollon tradition seems to have been pottery. Together with many unpainted and monochrome types, there appear the first geometrical bichrome patterns. Baskets continued to be very important and in fact they reached a climax both technically and artistically. The same is true of plaited sandals. Other innovations of this stage are the domestication of the turkey, the replacement of the spear-thrower with

FIG. 45 – *Naturalistic motifs of Mimbres black-on-white pottery. Fifth stage of the Mogollon tradition. After Cosgrove, 1932. Cf. p. 127.*

the bow and arrow, a shift to trough-like milling stones, numerous bone implements, the use of turquoise, the production of mosaics out of turquoise and shell, stone axes (rare), the first introduction of ceremonial buildings, and the use of feathers instead of furs for blankets. The dead continued to be buried in the flexed position.

The Modified Basketmaker stage prepared the way for the Developmental Pueblo stage (Pecos: Pueblo I and II), which has been placed in the period A.D. 700–1100. Already at the end of the earlier stage isolated houses appeared above ground and these now increased steadily in number so that by about 1100 they dominate the picture entirely. But it is not the case that this path was followed in the same way or at the same rate in all districts of what had become a rather vast cultural area. As might be expected in such a transition, local time lags and deviations happened that prevent exact chronological correlation; thus the dates mentioned above provide only a general framework. In the cultural complex that by 1100 included the whole area between southern Nevada and the Rio Grande in Colorado, and between the Colorado River in Utah and the upper course of the Little Colorado in Arizona and New Mexico, it is not surprising that variants developed—though these variants did not achieve their true importance until the following period. Common to all—to take one example—is the development of the kiva, the ceremonial meeting-house. While architecture changed fundamentally and pottery progressively—stimuli are supposed to have come from the Mississippi tradition of the eastern half of the present United States—shifts in other branches of art were much less significant. The most notable concern cotton growing and the appearance of true weaving. Basketry was practised perhaps even more intensively than before, though it lost a certain amount of ground to pottery and certain basket types died out. Apart from funnel-shaped and straight-sided smoking tubes, curved pipes in stone and clay were made. The flexed burial of the dead persists but these burials are easily distinguished from earlier ones, because skull deformation is now widely practised.

The peak of the Anasazi tradition was reached in the Great Pueblo stage (Pecos: Pueblo II) between 1100 and 1300. This culmination was not limited to the geographical spread, though indeed the Anasazi people achieved their greatest extension at this time and penetrated

View of a room in Pueblo Bonito, Chaco Canyon, N.M. The slightly trapezoidal opening of the door in the foreground is provided with two small benches. The regular flagstone masonry is typical of the Chaco Canyon region. Great Pueblo period, Anasazi tradition. *Cf. p. 119.*

Hohokam territory, reaching as far as the Mexican border. More important are the big villages which originated at this time with houses of several storeys and a wealth of architectural detail. Local groups are just as prominent in architecture and village planning as in pottery. The other crafts, however, display only minimal differences, possibly because they were able to draw upon solutions worked out earlier. PLATE P. 93 Weaving was further perfected, though the patterns used in basketry declined in quality. Outstanding were the objects made of shell and FIG. 42 turquoise, especially mosaics and turquoise inlays, suggesting that ideas were coming in from Meso-America. That an extensive trade flourished with these southern areas is shown by the copper bells and numerous parrots imported for religious purposes.

The end of the Great Pueblo stage brought important changes, whose real cause is still disputed. In the second half of the twelfth century the pueblos on the northern fringe of the territory were gradually abandoned at irregular intervals. Their population retreated to the Chaco Canyon where they seem to have been peacefully received by the established settlers, who also adhered to the Anasazi tradition. The original homeland, the San Juan district, was given up in the thirteenth century, as was the newly settled Hohokam area in the following century. Two main theories have been advanced to explain this retrenchment, in which the Anasazi tradition concentrated chiefly in the drainage area of the Little Colorado and Rio Grande as well as on the upper Gila River. One theory suggests that these migrations were provoked by a long dry period, which to judge by tree-rings took place between 1276 and 1299. A prolonged drought might have disastrous effects on economic life, which was largely based on dry farming and the flooded field system without much development of irrigation. But this would suggest that all areas were abandoned at the same time, or at least within this particular period. However, the majority of settlements in the Chaco Canyon were already given up before 1276 and the more northerly settlements even earlier. Other sites were only abandoned after 1299. This period of over one hundred years seems too long to be explained by the great drought. The other theory is that aggressive Athabascan tribes, the later Navaho and Apache, appeared, driving the settlers out. The characteristic fortress-like appearance of the Pueblos of the thirteenth and fourteenth centuries, evidence of burning, and signs of violent death seem to speak in favour of this hypothesis, but they are less common than one might have expected. It is hard to imagine that small nomadic groups were in a position to conquer such large settlements as Pueblo Bonito,

which had more than 1000 inhabitants. But the possibility remains that repeated plunderings of fields and the resulting food shortages forced a withdrawal from pueblos that otherwise could have been taken only after a long struggle. For the present at least, this theory seems to provide the best explanation of the changes that took place. With these changes we have already entered the Regressive Pueblo stage (Pecos: Pueblo IV), placed between 1300 and 1600. The pueblos, which in many cases can be called cities in this period, are often distributed around a central plaza. The pattern of these settlements shifts towards the end of this stage, when a scheme of parallel rows or 'streets' appears. Pottery had already undergone extensive changes during the Great Pueblo stage. Painting in several colours, which was diffused from the south, replaced the bichrome work; it was associated with realistic human and animal motifs. Both elements, which are assumed to derive from Mexico, were now diffused throughout the entire Anasazi district. Glazing, another achievement of the preceding period, became more common. Other changes are minor and need not be mentioned here.

In 1540 the first pueblos, those of the Zuñi, were taken by an expedition led by Coronado and incorporated into the Spanish Empire. But the true conquest and the resulting continuous contact with European culture began as late as 1589. The Historic Pueblo stage (Pecos: Pueblo V), which is reckoned from this point and lasts until the present day, will be considered later in this chapter.

At the beginning of this discussion it was pointed out that other cultures existed outside the bounds of these three great traditions. They have not yet or not quite reached the status of a tradition, primarily because of the state of our knowledge. First efforts in this direction have already been made, such as the positioning of the Hakataya tradition, which comprises the Patayan and Sinagua cultures and the Pioneer stage of the Hohokam tradition, as has been mentioned. This includes the two most important cultures of the western border

Pataya

lands. The Patayan culture was confined to the valley of the Colorado below the Grand Canyon, as is attested by its remains, dating from about A.D. 500 onwards. Since these people seem to have made many objects out of perishable materials, our knowledge of this culture is very fragmentary and a division into phases cannot be made. Among the culture traits are flood-farming for growing maize, the lack of permanent houses, huts made of branches and brushwood, stone-lined cooking pits, brown or red-on-brown pottery and cremation of the dead.

Sinagua

The Sinagua originally lived in the San Francisco Mountains of

FIG. 46 – *Naturalistic motifs of Mimbres black-on-white pottery. Fifth phase of the Mogollon tradition. After Cosgrove, 1932. Cf. p. 127.*

northern Arizona and later spread into the Verde Valley. Their first traces go back to about A.D. 400. Since individual phases have scarcely been distinguished, these conjectures can be ignored here. As in the Mogollon and Anasazi traditions the Indians relied on the sudden floods that filled the otherwise dry arroyos or watercourses to water the maize fields. Typical of the early period are brown monochrome pottery and deep pit dwellings. The picture changes markedly with the explosion of the Sunset crater about 1065. The masses of ash that were thrown out increased the fertility of the land so greatly that not only did the Sinagua who had left earlier return to the area around Flagstaff, Arizona, but Hohokam and Anasazi groups settled there as well, so that an intermingling of traditions and cultures took place. While the Hohokam influence, as revealed by typical houses and ball-courts, soon disappeared, many things were taken over from the Anasazi tradition, such as building in stone, houses above ground and pottery forms and patterns. Thus in the course of the twelfth century the Sinagua were absorbed into the Anasazi tradition, as the settlements in the Verde Valley show. At the end of the thirteenth century, after the abandonment of the Flagstaff area, a branch of the Sinagua seems to have pushed into the territory of the Hohokam tradition and to have fused with the indigenous population there.

Small groups

We know even less about two other cultures of the western borderlands. The Cohonina, who lived in pit dwellings south of the Rio Grande, seem closely linked to the Patayan culture, while the Prescott group in the upper Verde Valley and the Valley of Agua Fria has a connexion with the Sinagua. So far as can be determined at this point both seem to represent blends that may be regarded as further ramifications of the Hakataya tradition.

The northern area also contained some marginal groups of Southwestern type, such as the Fremont and Sevier cultures, which occupied all central and northern Utah. To describe them briefly one can say that they were strongly influenced by the Anasazi tradition, but either did not keep pace with many developments or else took them over very much later. Thus pit dwellings were characteristic until *ca.* A.D. 1100 and such important Anasazi features as the kiva and domesticated turkeys were lacking. For all practical purposes this amounted to a prolongation of the Modified Basketmaker stage. Finally it must be mentioned that in the east as well, particularly in south-western Texas, strong influences from the Southwest can be detected.

ART   It has already been noted that there has as yet been hardly any true art history of the North American Indians. Consequently, no style regions have been formed and only rarely have the characteristic products of the various regions been thrown into relief. But if we may single out ivory carving for the Arctic, wood carving for the Northwest and basketry for California as typical crafts in which the arts of these regions excelled, then for the Southwest three crafts or branches of art deserve special mention: architecture, wall-painting and pottery. Since they have been purposely omitted from the discussion so far, they can now be discussed en bloc.

Architecture   The beginnings of architecture in the Southwest were modest. If one disregards the brush huts of the Patayan, the sunken houses of the Basketmaker people must be regarded as the simplest. Here the walls, which inclined slightly inwards towards the top, were built of vertical beams so as to create an almost circular room. The interstices were filled with mud. The roof, which rested directly on the walls, was made of logs piled irregularly one on top of the other, so that it presented a somewhat mound-like shape. The interior was correspondingly simple, comprising mainly a fire pit to hold hot stones and storage pits of various types, which were sometimes lined with stone slabs and provided with a beehive-shaped mud covering. Storage pits of this kind were also established in caves and rock shelters, which were still often used for accommodation.

Pit houses   The next step in this development was the pit house that was widely diffused throughout the Southwest. Appearing in the Modified Basketmaker stage of the Anasazi tradition, these houses characterize the whole Mogollon tradition (except for the last stage) and the first three Hohokam stages. They are also found among the Cohonina

General view of Cliff Palace, Mesa Verde, Colo. This typical village of the Mesa Verde region, which originally comprised some 200 rooms rising in part to four storeys in height, lies under an overhanging cliff. No overall plan was employed; rather the village grew up haphazardly according to need. The round kivas were incorporated into the building mass. Great Pueblo period, Anasazi tradition. *Cf. p. 119.*

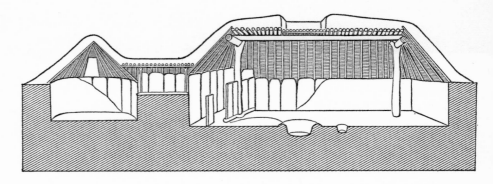

FIG. 47 – *Reconstruction of a pit house of the Modified Basketmaker stage, Anasazi tradition. The entrance is in the antechamber. The roof, which is supported by posts, is covered with branches, underbrush and earth. The walls are lined with upright stone slabs covered with plaster. The larger cavity in the floor is the fire-place, the smaller the sipapu. The smoke hole is in the centre of the roof over the fireplace. After Roberts, 1929. Cf. below.*

and the Sinagua, as well as in the Fremont culture and in Texas. What unites and what distinguishes the several cultures and traditions? First, the Hohokam dwellings are really sunken houses rather than pit houses, for they do not employ pit walls. But since the principle is ultimately the same, they can be included here. In the Modified Basketmaker stage the house plan was initially round, then oval and finally rectangular. It was rectangular also among the Hohokam, though in the Colonial and Sedentary stages the corners were rounded off. The first stage of the Mogollon tradition shows the geratest formal diversification; in order of frequency we find houses that are round, oval, irregular, kidney-shaped, D-shaped and (rarely) rectangular. From this plethora of forms the third stage selected two: rectangular plans appear in seventy per cent of the cases, while the rest are round. This proportion continues in the fourth stage. The simplest wall construction was that of the Mogollon tradition, which used the earthen walls of the pit. Only in the fourth stage were the walls customarily lined with adobe or mud plastering. The latter method re-appears in the houses of the Anasazi tradition, an indication that they were probably borrowed from the Mogollon. More common among the Anasazi was the lining of walls with vertically placed stone slabs, normally surmounted by several courses of adobe bricks. The walls of the Hohokam houses consisted of upright poles interwoven with branches, grass or reeds. As with the Sinagua houses, these walls

FIG. 47

were plastered with earth or mud. More problematic is the question of roof construction, which is preserved only in rare cases. In the Modified Basketmaker stage the roof took the form of a full or truncated cone supported by four posts. The roofs of the Pioneer Hohokam stage were similar, as were, in some instances, those of the first Mogollon stage. The conical roofs of the houses of the latter frequently required a central post for additional support. In the third and fourth Mogollon stages roofs were either truncated-conical with four corner posts or double-pitched with from one to three ridge beams; this first method of construction was used during the Colonial and Sedentary stages of the Hohokam tradition. The roofs of the Sinagua houses were flat. Almost all the pit houses mentioned had long covered entrances built according to various techniques. In the Modified Basketmaker stage the entrance was provided with an anteroom. Then towards the end of this stage the entrance became so small that it lost its purpose and was replaced by a hatch in the roof. Fireplaces were fixed either in the centre (Anasazi, Mogollon 1–3) or near the entrance (Hohokam 3–4). Storage pits were especially characteristic of the houses of the Mogollon tradition. The Modified Basketmaker people kept their stores in rooms above ground, usually situated behind the dwelling pits.

While the practice of digging pit houses certainly grew from the Cochise base and was probably perfected in the Mogollon tradition, to all appearances the development of houses above ground belongs exclusively to the Anasazi tradition. As a rule, when in later times these houses appear outside the bounds of the tradition (Classical Hohokam, Mogollon 5, Sinagua after A.D. 1100), the presence of Anasazi influence can definitely be demonstrated. In order to clarify the architecture above ground, therefore, we must deal with its development within the Anasazi tradition. The transitions took place during the Modified Basketmaker stage, primarily towards the end, and during the following Developmental Pueblo stage. The models for the first houses above ground were apparently the storage rooms which had been in use for some time, for like the latter the walls of the new dwelling houses, which were made of sticks with the intervals filled with mud, had a batter towards the top. Later these walls became entirely vertical and the intervals were filled with masonry. In the next phase the walls were built exclusively of stone. This development was completed as early as A.D. 800, though some districts clung to older fashions. While the first houses built above ground stood quite close together, though still separated by a narrow space, later they were erected wall to wall. Omitting special variants, this was the

Houses above ground

general picture of a pueblo village during the ninth century: a double row of linked rectangular houses placed above ground and in a curve so as to form a cresent. The walls in the back row were often more crudely built, while the front walls displayed horizontally placed stone slabs. The back rooms were used exclusively for storing provisions, while the front ones could serve either the same purpose or as living quarters. Otherwise the Indians lived in pit houses dug in front of the two surface rows; in other cases these pit houses were used for ceremonial functions. This triple series continued to be standard practice until the end of the stage, except that in later times life was carried on exclusively above ground and the pit house was turned into a ceremonial chamber, the kiva.

The kiva
FIGS. 48, 49

The kiva, which has survived to our own day, has indeed undergone changes of detail in the course of its thousand-year history, but the basic principles have remained the same, showing without doubt its derivation from the pit house. The usual norm was and still is a round plan with a diameter of 13 to 17 feet. Rectangular kivas were present during the Great Pueblo stage in the Kayenta district and later diffused over a larger area, but their interior arrangements were generally

PLATE P. 105

FIG. 48 – *Ground-plan of a kiva of the Great Pueblo stage, Anasazi tradition. Lowry Pueblo, Colorado. After Martin, Quimby and Collier, 1947. Cf. above.*

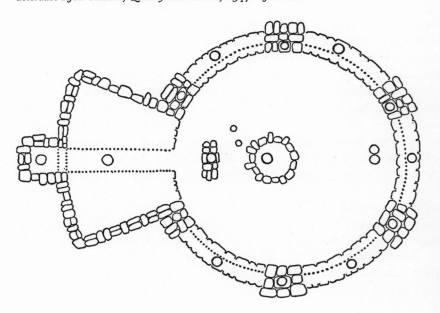

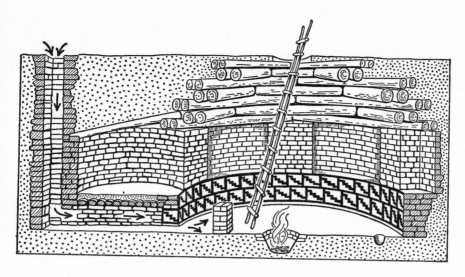

FIG. 49 – *Reconstruction of a kiva of the Great Pueblo phase, Anasazi tradition. The shaft at the left turning 90° at the bottom is the ventilator; before the opening in the kiva is the deflector, which is aligned with the fireplace in the middle of the room and the sipapu. The roof consists of logs overlapping to form a central entrance hatchway, which is accessible by a ladder. The walls consist of stones covered with plaster. After Roberts, 1929, and Martin, Quimby and Collier, 1947. Cf. p. 116.*

the same as those with the round plan. The Indians built the walls of the kiva in stone and assembled the roof, which was supported on masonry piers let into the walls, from logs laid one on top of the other. With its upper corners projecting somewhat above the surface of the earth, the roof also included the entrance, from which the chamber was reached by means of a ladder. The former covered entrance to the pit house became a side chamber, under which an L-shaped shaft brought fresh air into the kiva. Some distance from the interior opening of the shaft stands a small diagonal masonry wall known as the 'deflector', a baffle preventing the stream of air from putting out the fire in the central fireplace. As a direct continuation of the line formed by the ventilator opening, the deflector and the fireplace, there lies near the opposite wall a hole in the floor known as the *sipapu*, a symbolic entrance to the world of the spirits. This feature was also anticipated by the pit houses. Finally, we must mention a continuous masonry bench along the walls, interrupted only by the projecting piers.

During the Great Pueblo stage a special type of kiva appeared in the Chaco and Mesa Verde area. Apart from their large size—the dia-

Wall-painting, Kuaua, N.M. In this detail from a larger tableau concerned with sowing, rain and the fertility of the soil we see (beginning at the left) the following scenes: a wild goose with rain pouring from its mouth; a masked human figure bearing a feather crown and holding a staff—this figure appears to be the 'lightning maker'; a fish projecting rain on one side and a rainbow on the other, leading to a black eagle, from whose beak comes a lightning bolt and a stream of seeds falling to earth; in the stream of seeds flies an arrow-head or a bat, which again distributes rain. Moisture also comes from the pot beneath the eagle, from which a lightning bolt projects as well. At the far right are foot-prints, arrow-heads and red stones that are connected with a ritual competition. The painting is unrelated stylistically to those of the Jeddito Valley. Layer G-26, south-west corner, kiva III, Kuaua, N. M. Approximately sixteenth century, Regressive Pueblo period, Anasazi tradition. *Cf. p. 125.*

meter measures some 60–95 feet—these buildings show a number of peculiarities. Ringed by small rooms on the surface, they possess a staircase and free-standing piers to support the roof. The stone-lined cavities in the floor seem to have been covered with planks so that they could serve as foot drums, an arrangement that can still be seen in a kiva at Acoma.

At the beginning of the Great Pueblo stage about A.D. 1100 pueblo architecture was fully developed. But this is only homogeneous in its basic principles, for many regional variations occur, of which the three most important will be described here. The best architecture of this period is found in the Chaco Canyon area and in the districts under its influence in northern New Mexico and north-eastern Arizona. Pueblo Bonito, which will serve as an example here, is one of the largest settlements. Actually the Pueblo took the form of one vast semicircular building that was closed on the normally open south side by a single straight row of rooms. While this additional wing was only one storey high, the main complex originally rose to four storeys, each storey being set back by one unit in depth so that a step-like effect was produced. The walls, which taper gradually towards the top, have a core of mud and stones lined on both sides with courses of flagstones. These courses are so well built that a knife blade can scarcely be inserted between them. The horizontally placed roof beams are hewn square. Over them lies a layer of thin sticks, followed by willow mats, wood shavings and finally earth, which constitute the floor of the next storey. The rooms are fairly large (about 180 square feet) and from six to ten feet high. It is estimated that the approximately 800 rooms, which are linked by large, usually trapezoidal doorways, would have accommodated some 1200 people at the height of the village's prosperity. The windowless inner rooms served for the storage of supplies and the preparation of the maize, while the bright outer rooms were used for living quarters. The numerous kivas were either dug in the central plaza between the main block and the enclosing wing or joined to the building mass. Originally various entrances opened on to the central plaza from the outside, but in the course of time these were gradually walled up, leaving only a small opening in the south side, suggesting fear of attack by nomadic groups.

The typical pueblos of the Mesa Verde region in south-western Colorado were built in the shelter of overhanging cliffs. A good example of these cliff dwellings, as they are called, is Cliff Palace with its more than 200 rooms and kivas. While the layout of Pueblo Bonito implies planning, Cliff Palace seems to have grown up haphazardly through

Chaco Canyon

PLATE P. 105

PLATE P. 108

Mesa Verde

PLATE P. 113

Wall-painting, Pottery Mound, N. M. The opening of a tunnel appears in the centre. To the left of this is a woman with a crane standing behind her. Over this group hang chains of shell and coral, as well as folded textiles. To the right of the opening sits a man with white maize plants sprouting from his rainbow cap. Behind him is a parrot and above the sky with clouds. A basket with chains stands between the man and the crane. A man sitting on the basket was partially obliterated by the later introduction of the tunnel. Some echoes of Style II of the Jeddito Valley are discernible, but the scenic character of this style seems to be absent, so that this fresco occupies a place apart. Layer 1, west wall, kiva 2, Pottery Mound, Puerco Valley, N. M. Approximately A.D. 1400, Regressive Pueblo period, Anasazi tradition. *Cf. p. 125.*

constant new building. It too had four storeys, but the rooms were smaller (about 65 square feet) and lower (5 feet). If used for living purposes at all, these rooms evidently served only for sleeping, other activities being conducted on the roof terraces or in the plaza. The wall construction favoured horizontally placed, carefully worked stones, which are best described as 'loaf-shaped'. As in the Chaco Canyon district, the walls were carefully plastered on both sides. A special feature, however, are the windowless towers of several storeys built on various ground plans; their significance is not yet understood. These towers appear either in the pueblos themselves or set apart.

A third building type had its centre in the Kayenta region of Arizona. *Kayenta* The unplanned settlements, which form a loose agglomeration of

Wall-painting, Pottery Mound, N. M. Four grasshoppers or cicadas climb on flower stalks from the earth to the sky, which is indicated by stylized clouds. The meaning of this painting and its stylistic classification are uncertain. Layer 1, north wall, kiva 1, Pottery Mound, Puerco Valley, N. M. Approximately A.D. 1400, Regressive Pueblo period, Anasazi tradition. *Cf. p. 125.*

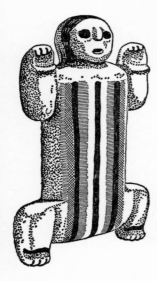

FIG. 50 – *Sandstone figure with stripes painted in black, orange, green and blue. It is thought that this example, which so far remains unique, may represent a kachina. If so, it is the oldest known figure of this kind. Regressive Pueblo stage, Anasazi tradition. Found in a kiva near Vernon, Arizona. After Archaeology, vol. 13, (1960), p. 289. Cf. p. 136.*

single houses, were situated both under cliffs and in the open. The technique of the Kayenta buildings, which was inferior to that of the other regions, involved stones combined with a good deal of mud to form irregular layouts. In size and height the rooms are intermediate between those of the other two regions discussed. Apart from the kivas, rectangular ceremonial rooms were also built above ground, a door replacing the ventilator of the underground forerunner.

These three styles, however, by no means apply to all the Great Pueblo villages, few of which were as large as the examples we have described. Many smaller communities flourished, whose architecture scarcely differed from that of the preceding stage. But a trend towards agglomeration was clearly discernible throughout the period and the more impressive house and settlement type spread to the Hohokam, Mogollon and Sinagua, where it exercised decisive influence.

Changes in the Regressive Pueblo period were relatively slight. Settlements continued to be built in the same way, but seldom rose above three storeys. The central plaza, which was usually found in the fourteenth century, made way for a row arrangement with streets or parallel plazas and these are characteristic of the sixteenth century. Only rarely did good masonry appear and standards were considerably lower than in the earlier epoch. Masonry generally combined irregular layers of big stones with plenty of mud for mortar; in some cases mud alone was used. We have now reached the transition to the architecture of the historical stage, which will be further discussed below.

Wall-painting The second main artistic achievement of the prehistoric Southwest, wall-painting, was a monopoly of the Anasazi tradition. Wall-paintings can be traced back to the second half of the Developmental Pueblo phase; and the fact that in this period they are only known from the northern and eastern parts of the San Juan district may be due to the better conditions for preservation found there. The few examples that we have of early wall-painting come almost exclusively from kiva walls. Actually they amount to little more than an ornamental elaboration of the boundary line separating two coloured surfaces. This type of work is also common in the following stage, but geometrical motifs freed from their attachment to the boundaries between the coloured surfaces play a greater role. The motifs themselves are not an innovation, for they were invented in the preceding period. What is new, however, is the appearance of men and animals in the repertory. These are quite clumsily done and are limited to isolated figures unrelated to one another.

The great period of wall-painting was apparently the Regressive Pueblo phase, not only because of the wealth of examples, but also because of the execution in which scenic representations and interrelated compositions overshadow all other features. Four great find complexes belong to this stage: Kuaua in the Rio Grande Valley, Awatovi and Kawaika-a in the Jeddito Valley, which belong to the drainage area of the Little Colorado, and Pottery Mound on the Rio Puerco in the drainage region of the Rio Grande. The presence of several hundred wall-paintings in each of these sites is due to the fact that the walls were provided with new layers of mud covering at unknown intervals and for unknown reasons; on each occasion new designs were painted. Thus as many as one hundred superimposed layers of paintings have been found. This has facilitated the study of style sequences, which have proved to be technically homogeneous; the colours were either applied with a stiff brush or dabbed on with a finger in *fresco secco* technique. The colour range was astonishingly broad, including yellow, blue, green, red, pink, orange, cinnobar, purple, brown, reddish brown, black, white and grey. Almost all colours were non-organic. In the Jeddito Valley, where the material has been well published, the figures, patterns and the like are often provided with black, white or (uncommonly) red contour lines; these always appear where two colour areas impinge. But the colour areas were not first marked out and then filled in, as one would assume. Instead large areas of colour were laid on initially and then the edges were over-painted with thin lines. Within the pattern overpainting is common also, especially for details of the figures.

In the Jeddito Valley scholars have identified four style groups, which are in turn divided into sub-styles. Style IV, the oldest of these, shows a single central feature on the wall that does not fill the whole surface. In the first sub-style this feature is always geometrical and frequently comprises a circle with decoration confined only to a small sector which was partitioned off. A similar phenomenon appears in pottery, especially the Four Mile Polychrome type. Primitive naturalism is the hallmark of the somewhat later sub-style 2; chronologically it parallels sub-style 1 of Style III. This latter style is characterized by

the fact that a big area is surrounded by a contour line and completely filled with a basic colour. In sub-style 1 this field is decorated with a purely geometrical pattern in the form of diagonal bands, interwoven meanders and the like. Sub-style 2 of Style III, which is later than 1 but contemporaneous with 3 and with Style I, is characterized by decidedly flamboyant patterns. The artists tended to arrange a wealth of volutes, scrolls, feather-like designs, rosettes and zigzag lines around one or more circular central features. Similarities with Mexican sun designs are found in these patterns, which recur in the motifs of the Sikyatki Polychrome. Sub-style 3 of Style III, however, is much quieter and more symmetrical with few frills.

While the patterns of Styles III and IV are largely geometric, this is not true of Styles I and II. Typical of Style I is its use of a continuous or broken band as a kind of ground line for the figures or elements to stand upon. Men and animals are presented in a very static manner and no action appears in paintings of Style I. The scenes are well balanced and often reach an almost perfect bilateral symmetry. By contrast the most recent Style II not only lacks the ground line, but the whole style has been radically transformed. All figures are found in full movement, despite the conventional stiffness that is a property of all Anasazi painting. Battle scenes occur frequently. The general layout and the execution, which often omits particular details, suggest sudden inspiration, in contrast to Style I, which seems to be planned down to the last detail.

The wall-paintings of Kuaua, in so far as they are known, are best PLATE P. 118 connected with Style II, the latest of the Jeddito Valley group, but they show many individual variations. Among these are the frequent representation of maize plants, and of rain and lightning. Fewer scenes are found, but more continuous rows of figures, which often show no relation to one another; this style does not appear in Awatovi and Kawaika-a. Of the numerous paintings from the Pottery Mound PLATES PP. 120, 121 only a few are known so far. They suggest that similarities existed with Styles I and II of the Jeddito Valley, as well as with paintings from Kuaua.

Above: pottery bowl in the geometric style of the Mimbres black-on-white type. Found at Mimbres Valley, N. M. Fifth stage of the Mogollon tradition. *Diameter 22.9 cm. Southwest Museum, Los Angeles, Calif. Cf. p. 127.*

Below: pottery vessel of the Sikyatki Polychrome type. Found at Jeddito Valley, Ariz. Regressive Pueblo period, Anasazi tradition. *Diameter 70 cm. Southwest Museum, Los Angeles, Calif. Cf. p. 130.*

FIG. 51 – *Thick-walled pottery bowl with red decoration on a light brown ground. Repetitive animal patterns are characteristic of the Sedentary stage of the Hohokam tradition. Found in south-western Arizona. Southwest Museum, Los Angeles. Photograph courtesy of H. von Winning. Cf. p. 128.*

Pottery The third branch of art characteristic of the Southwest is pottery. This art incorporates fine nuances that permit scholars to distinguish the whole panoply of sequences with their ramifications, stages and phases. As 'index fossils' it is not surprising that ceramic types have been intensively studied so that many specialized monographs exist on their technique, classification and style. Since only the specialist needs to know all the fine distinctions and the many types, only the main lines will be traced and illustrated with a few individual types.

Mogollon The relatively continuous development in the Mogollon tradition begins in the first stage, characterized by bowls and spherical vessels with narrow necks in red or brown. While the earliest vessels seem to have been moulded from a lump of clay, the coil technique was soon introduced, with the traces of the coils obliterated by scraping. Only towards the end of the stage were the coils on the neck occasionally left untouched. During the same period blackening of vessels through firing in a reducing atmosphere gained popularity. In the little-known Mogollon 2 stage the existing types apparently continued to be produced. They were supplemented by a red-on-brown bichrome, with an angular geometric decoration executed with broad lines. This development continues in the third stage; red-on-brown remains the main type of decoration, but it now involves fine lines and complicated geometric decoration made up of triangles, zigzag lines, hatchings and so forth. The form of the vessels remains relatively constant and the undecorated types of the preceding stage continue to be produced. Innovations of the third stage are plastic decorations made by punctation and the use of slip. At the end of this stage and in the following one a red-on-white type came into use in the southern districts, though the patterns do not differ from those of earlier times. In the fourth stage red-on-white was the leading colour combination. Simultaneously, however, certain influences became evident, especially from the Anasazi tradition, as witnessed by the black-on-white types appearing at this time in the Mimbres district and the 'corrugated' vessels. During the fifth stage almost the whole area was incorporated into the Anasazi tradition. Only in the Mimbres region did a special development persist that is particularly noticeable in ceramics. The old uncomplicated red and brown ware originated by the Mogollon tradition continued, while the corrugated types show the Anasazi influence. But all these types were overshadowed by the Mimbres black-on-white, artistically the finest pottery produced in the Southwest. The type consists almost exclusively of bowls, of which two-thirds were decorated with geometric patterns. Triangles, zigzags and meanders were painted with the finest brushwork and with an excellent sense of composition and balance. This would suffice to assure the fame of these ceramics, if they were not surpassed by the other third of the production, which features stylized naturalistic forms. The repertory comprises birds, quadrupeds, fish, insects and, in a good many cases, human figures, shown both singly and in groups. The sensitive line and individual handling of each piece would redound to any artist's credit. The source of this sudden and highly skilled use of naturalistic forms has not yet been ascertained.

PLATE P. 124

FIGS. 44, 45, 46

The Hohokam tradition is often proposed as the origin of or stimulus for the Mimbres pottery, in as much as naturalistic motifs had long been at home here. From the beginning, that is since the Pioneer stage, the spiral coiling technique was in use with the coils disguised by the paddle and anvil method, which is otherwise unknown in the Southwest. Monochrome vessels, mostly bowls and pitchers, were light brown, grey or red. The bichrome decoration appearing soon afterwards was initially red-on-grey, later red-on-light-brown. Geometric ornaments with lines, spirals and hatchings appear in all types, while naturalistic motifs were confined to the red-on-light-

Hohokam

FIG. 52 – *Thick-walled pottery vessel in the form of a bighorn sheep (?) with red painting on a light brown ground. Sedentary stage, Hohokam tradition. Found in Arizona. Southwest Museum, Los Angeles. Photograph courtesy of H. von Winning. Cf. p. 128.*

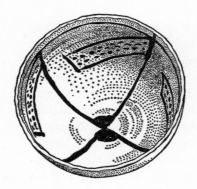

FIG. 53 – *Pottery bowl of the Lino black-on-white type. Modified Basketmaker stage, Anasazi tradition. Found in Arizona. Southwest Museum, Los Angeles. Photograph courtesy of H. von Winning. Cf. below.*

brown ware and are consequently later than the geometric decoration. Finally, this stage saw the appearance of the first polychrome painting of the Southwest: yellow was introduced into one of the red-on-grey types. For the following stages of the Hohokam tradition red-on-light-brown was the dominant colour scheme. The use of hatchings, spirals and naturalistic motifs was typical of the Colonial stage. The ornaments, mostly rather small, were often repeated. Among the naturalistic motifs, birds, snakes and insects reflect the animal world of the surrounding desert. The human figure commonly occurs, though it is

FIGS. 51, 52 severely stylized and often hardly recognizable. In the Sedentary stage the interlacing patterns often recall those of textiles. Naturalistic motifs continued in popularity. Their importance decreased markedly, however, in the Classic stage, when the practice of ceramic painting —still carried out in the red-on-light-brown tradition—underwent a qualitative eclipse. Irregular brush strokes and angular decoration characterize this period. The pottery of the Salado, who appeared at this time in the Hohokam territory, belongs to the Anasazi tradition; its polychrome decoration stands out against a red ground.

Anasazi Anasazi was the last of the three main traditions to produce ceramics, beginning at the start of the Modified Basketmaker stage about A.D. 400. Like many other achievements of this period the idea of pottery seems to have come from outside, apparently from the Mogollon tradition. But a fundamental transformation quickly followed and only the coiling technique—later developing into true spiral coiling—which lasted until the end, and the practice of scraping continued to indicate its origin. Undecorated vessels were grey and often left unsmoothed at the neck as in the Mogollon tradition. The

FIG. 53 decoration of the bichrome pottery, which was black-on-grey or else white- or red-on-orange, was uncomplicatedly geometric, usually with a broad-line decoration. In the Developmental Pueblo stage many innovations appear. The simple grey vessels were produced more abundantly, but were supplemented by corrugated types in which the spiralling coils were no longer obliterated on the exterior, but were emphasized by finger impressions. With the exception of the Alkali Ridge in south-eastern Utah in the first half of the stage, the bichrome pottery henceforth was black-on-white. The more skilfully executed FIG. 54 decoration remained geometric, displaying spirals, step motifs, meanders and hatchings. The work of the Great Pueblo stage has geometric ornament too. As in architecture regional variations now appear that follow separate paths of development. Typical of the black-on-white pottery of the Chaco branch are triangles and rectangular FIG. 56 spirals. The patterns were delimited with forceful lines and filled with fine hatching. Likewise, the pottery of Mesa Verde in the same colours displays hatching, though it is much coarser. Also typical here are black surfaces and step patterns. As a further distinction one should note that the black colour of the Mesa Verde district is of vegetable origin, while that of the Chaco area is mineral. More varied is the pottery of the Kayenta district. The black-on-white types FIG. 55 display negative zigzag lines, very fine, dense hatchings through which the ground is hardly distinguishable, and interlocking step patterns. The Kayenta district also produced black decoration on an orange or red ground. In all regions, however, corrugated pottery continued in FIG. 57 use. Apart from generally diffused shapes, certain ones are restricted to particular districts, such as the straight-walled, flat-bottomed pitchers of the Mesa Verde region.

The first polychrome pottery appears towards the end of the stage in

FIG. 54 – *Pottery vessel of the Tuyasan black-on-red type, possibly representing a highly stylized bird. Developmental Pueblo stage, Anasazi tradition. Found in Arizona. Southwest Museum, Los Angeles. Photograph courtesy of H. von Winning. Cf. above.*

the Chaco and Kayenta region, and later dominates the ceramics of the Regressive Pueblo stage, though regional specialities played a role as well. Thus with its Jeddito white-on-yellow type the Hopi district in north-eastern Arizona continued the old Kayenta tradition.

PLATE P. 124 The partly geometrical, partly naturalistic motifs of the Sikyatki Polychrome are red and black on a yellowish ground. With their abstraction of men and animals they rank among the most interesting ceramic products of the Southwest; they can almost be compared with the Mimbres bowls. The glaze colours of the Cibola district in eastern Arizona and western New Mexico, which together with many poly-chrome types form the picture of pottery there, had a lead basis, rarely one of copper. Similar glaze colours appeared in the Rio Grande district of central New Mexico, though in this region the colours were used within the context of the numerous polychrome types. Here birds and human heads appear together with geometric motifs, while in the Cibola district the decoration was mostly geometric. In everyday wares the corrugated types, though numerous at the outset, gradually gave way to simple grey vessels.

ETHNOLOGY Of all the old cultures of the Southwest the Anasazi tradition has shown an especial capacity for survival: the so-called Pueblo culture is its direct offspring. The villages that are still inhabited, of which some go back to pre-Spanish times, are built in the Anasazi manner. In the west the walls are of stone with adobe mortar; in the east (in the Rio Grande Valley) they are executed in hand-made adobe bricks. But only a few settlements are built in several storeys and Taos, the northernmost of them, is unique in reaching five storeys. Two types of settlement have continued until the present day: in one

FIG. 55 – *Pottery vessel of the Tuyasan Black-on-white type. It shows the typical zigzag and meander of the Kayenta region. Developmental Pueblo stage, Anasazi tradition. Found in Arizona. Southwest Museum, Los Angeles. Photograph courtesy of H. von Winning. Cf. p. 129.*

FIG. 56 – *Pottery vessel with two small suspension lugs. The Tularosa Black-on-white type is particularly characteristic of the style of the Cibola region. Great Pueblo stage, Anasazi tradition. Found in New Mexico. Southwest Museum, Los Angeles. Photograph courtesy of H. von Winning. Cf. p. 129.*

case the 'houses' cluster around one or more plazas, in the other they are distributed along several parallel streets or plazas. The kivas also persist in these layouts, though a good many of them—particularly in the west and in the Tewa pueblos—are rectangular, some even being built above ground. Since the clans and societies gather in them to plan ceremonies and festivals, they remain the religious focus of village life today, just as they probably were in pre-European times.

PLATE P. 132

Despite the semblance of uniformity, a quality that marks other branches of art as well, some significant differences exist in Pueblo culture. These are expressed in the diversity of language; the four speech groups represented make mutual comprehension impossible. Several attempts have been made to draw a distinction between the western pueblos in the desert (Hopi, Zuñi and the Keresan villages of Acoma and Laguna) and the villages in the Rio Grande Valley. Such a distinction is indeed valid, but closer examination shows that no sharp boundaries exist, only fluid transitions. Many of the modern differences, particularly in social forms and religion, are due to Spanish influences, which were most effective in the Rio Grande Valley, while the Hopi living farther west were hardly touched. It is doubtful, however, whether the Hopi are entirely faithful to the forms of pre-European times. We cannot undertake to describe fully the details of

FIG. 57 – *Pottery bowl of the Tularosa Corrugated type. The unsmoothed coils of the outer wall are reddish brown with white decoration. The smooth inner wall is black. Great Pueblo stage, Anasazi tradition. Found in Arizona. Southwest Museum, Los Angeles. Photograph courtesy of H. von Winning. Cf. p. 129.*

Air view of Pueblo Acoma, one of the oldest surviving villages of the Southwest with a history of at least a thousand years. It occupies a defensive position on an isolated sandstone mesa. The stone buildings rising as high as three storeys are arranged along parallel 'streets'. The rectangular kivas are incorporated into the buildings. The big building in the right foreground is a mission church, the oldest parts of which date from before 1644. In 1948 Pueblo Acoma had 1447 inhabitants. *Cf. p. 131.*

Pueblo culture nor all the distinctions between groups and areas, but by concentrating on extremes we can at least illustrate the range of variation.

One extreme is represented by the Hopi, who live in the west. They follow a strictly matrilocal organization; that is, after marriage the husband joins his wife's group, which holds title to the dwellings and land, while the clan has jurisdiction over the ceremonies and the physical objects related to them, including the kiva. The societies are closely linked with the clans, for their leaders are also the clan priests. This office is inherited within the clan, as is that of the village chief, who must come from a particular clan. An exception is provided by the medicine societies into which anyone can be received who has been healed by a member. The societies regulate the lengthy ceremonies that take place throughout the year in which masked dancers personify rain and cloud spirits. *Hopi*

In the pueblos of the Rio Grande the older forms shine through only dimly. Changes were particularly marked in the north, where contacts were close with the non-pueblo tribes of the Southeast and the Plains. Even economic life was different, for irrigation was possible on the Rio Grande, while conditions in the west permitted dry farming only. Important differences also exist in the social and religious spheres. Matrilinearity diminishes more and more, disappearing entirely in Taos in the north. *Rio Grande*

Similar changes affect the inherited rights of clan participation: membership and offices are open to all, including the double village chieftainship, where the yearly election together with the titles and attibutes reflect Spanish influence. Since masked dances were officially forbidden in colonial times, they could be held only inside the kivas together with religious ceremonies. This custom is still maintained today and no outsider is allowed to see them. By contrast, all the public dances, in which men and women alike participate, are performed without masks.

The many old crafts that have survived may be classified under two headings: secular and ceremonial art. While the first group is found in almost all pueblos, the second, so far as we can determine, is largely restricted to the west, especially the Hopi and Zuñi villages. *Crafts*

Apart from pottery, weaving and basketry, the secular crafts include work in turquoise and silver. The latter skill was introduced from Mexico only after the end of Spanish colonial rule. Silver and turquoise ornaments are still made, though generally for the tourist trade. Competition from modern industrial materials is destroying the native arts of weaving and basketry; the only sizeable production today comes from the Hopi villages. There basket trays are made by the women and display geometric and stylized naturalistic motifs in bright colours. By contrast the men do the weaving in the kivas. The geometric decoration of blankets and fabrics derives from basketry patterns.

Pottery Unlike the other crafts, pottery, which is done by women, still flourishes in almost all pueblos. The various villages, or at least small groupings of them, show distinct local preferences in form and decoration. Patterns may be either geometric or naturalistic; on one hand they reveal the persistence of ancient Indian traditions and on the other European—mostly Spanish—influences. The unpainted pottery of the northern Rio Grande pueblos (Taos, Picuris) is smoked or decorated with appliqué work; it has a high mica content. Monochrome red and black vessels are made in San Juan, Santa Clara and San Ildefonso. The potters of Tesuque and Santo Domingo, who used to produce a black-on-light-brown ware, now work exclusively for the tourist trade. The small figures and vessels are painted with commercial colours after firing. This style has also spread to Jemez. Cochiti, however, has retained the old style, typified by geometric and naturalistic decoration. The southern Keresan pueblos between Zia and Acoma form a group together with the Tiwa pueblo Isleta. In their pottery, which can only be distinguished by details, a white ground sets off the red and orange decoration. Black is also used, though normally only to separate the colour areas. Motifs include straight PLATE P. 135 and curved lines as well as flowers and birds. Zuñi pots also display a white ground. The geometric and naturalistic patterns are red or black. Especially characteristic are rosettes, small birds with long tails and deer that have a red stripe from heart to muzzle. Among the Hopi painted vessels now come only from the villages of the First Mesa; they have a cream ground with red and black decoration. This type was introduced at the end of the nineteenth century by Nampeyo after she had accompanied her husband on excavation and seen old pottery, especially that of the Sikyatki type. Even today the patterns often reflect this old style; they have strongly stylized birds and feathers, though kachina figures also occur. Nampeyo's is not the only example of a single potter reviving a seemingly dying craft. At the beginning of the 1920s another woman, Maria Martinez of San Ildefonso, produced black vessels with a polished decoration against a mat ground. This style, soon a collector's item, has spread and is now produced in some of the neighbouring pueblos.

Although we have distinguished between secular and religious art,

Large pottery vessel with polychrome decoration. The style shows strong European influence, notably in the plant motifs and the cock. Acoma, late nineteenth century. *Height 28.5 cm. Museum für Völkerkunde, Hamburg. Cf. p. 134.*

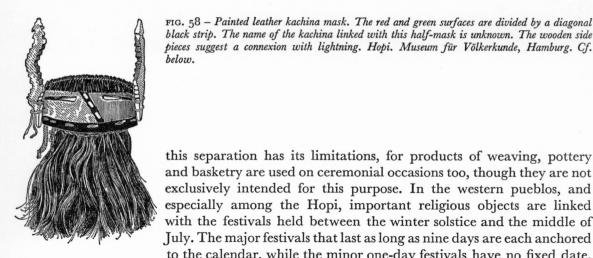

FIG. 58 – *Painted leather kachina mask. The red and green surfaces are divided by a diagonal black strip. The name of the kachina linked with this half-mask is unknown. The wooden side pieces suggest a connexion with lightning. Hopi. Museum für Völkerkunde, Hamburg. Cf. below.*

this separation has its limitations, for products of weaving, pottery and basketry are used on ceremonial occasions too, though they are not exclusively intended for this purpose. In the western pueblos, and especially among the Hopi, important religious objects are linked with the festivals held between the winter solstice and the middle of July. The major festivals that last as long as nine days are each anchored to the calendar, while the minor one-day festivals have no fixed date. Common to all, however, is the simulation of kachinas by masked dancers. The kachinas are conceived as spirits that bring rain and fertility, delighting men with their dancing. They are generally regarded as benevolent, though they may occasionally harm people. Kachinas may be personified animals or plants; sometimes they are ancestors or divine messengers, sometimes personified souls of the gods or assistants to them. The Hopi pantheon comprises between 32 and 36 gods, though most are not depicted in masks. Another group are the Wawarus kachinas who incite men to compete in races. There are some 300 kachinas in all, of which 30, the Mong kachinas, must appear at every major festival. Their task is to carry to the gods the prayers and requests men vouchsafe to them during the dances.

The many kachinas can be distinguished from one another by their characteristic features. Dress helps in making preliminary distinctions, such as between the female and the much more numerous male kachinas. But the commonest forms are the masks, which are mostly made of leather or wood and which can be classified into five basic types. Within these types individual figures can be recognized through the shape of the eyes and mouth, through the head-dress, and (less commonly) through the beard and nose. But the surest signpost is the painting of the masks. Here the strong penchant for painting found among the Pueblo Indians comes to the fore; this has already been noted in pottery, where it goes back to early times. The painting embodies the basic symbolism of the masks, for the fact that each of the six colours is linked to one of the six world directions (including up and down) permits the artist to define the kachinas' point of origin. Other

Kachinas

FIG. 50

FIG. 58

important identifying markers appear on the cheeks and forehead, more rarely on the mouth of the masks; these include celestial symbols of geometric types, plants, animal tracks and fertility charms.

From what has been said it should be obvious that intensive study is needed to tell the many kachinas apart in the dance ceremonies and to recognize their specific meaning. In this connexion the kachina dolls—sometimes incorrectly identified with the kachinas themselves— are helpful. At the end of every festival masked dancers distribute them to the children present; generally they are made by the father or by an uncle who is charged with teaching the children, following matrilinear custom. The kachina dolls are not toys, but serve the needs of religious instruction, for the children learn to distinguish the various spirits from them. (The affinities with certain modern educational techniques are obvious.) At home the dolls are hung on walls or from rafters so that they may serve as a constant reminder of the lessons learned. In this way they are available not only to the child who actually received the gift, but also to his brothers, sisters and playmates. The older dolls, which are often made of cottonwood, show only a few carved details and are often rigid and stiff. Here the painting is most important and it corresponds exactly to that of the kachina impersonators themselves. However, since the kachina dolls have become a favourite of collectors the style has undergone a change. The dolls made today are much more lively—they are often shown in dancing positions—and consequently they are more attuned to European taste. Religious art is not confined solely to kachina masks and dolls. Many other objects, sometimes the speciality of particular regions, belong in this category, such as the figures of the Zuñi war gods with their abstract, post-like appearance—one of the rare Pueblo approaches to sculpture. The rest of religious art is painted; examples include dance rattles, boards carried on the head, paired dancing staffs, altar tablets, and sand paintings placed before the altar in the kivas.

The last-named art finds its highest development among the neighbouring Navaho. Here the paintings are executed not in kivas, which are unknown, but in huts, the hogans—in some cases in specially

PLATES PP. 139, 141

FIG. 59 – *Wooden figure of a twin war god. The vertically projecting part probably represents a feather cylinder attached to the navel; at the same time it is a symbol of the sipapu, the entrance to the underworld. Zuñi. Staatliches Museum für Völkerkunde, Berlin. Cf. above.*

built hogans that are bigger than the usual type. The occasions for making sand paintings are various, but they are mostly connected with illness, bad dreams and similar problems. A particular ceremony is prescribed to suit the occasion; then the proceedings may last as long as four days. Each of these ritual events focuses on the experiences of a mythical hero, who once brought certain songs, paintings and activities to mankind, after the gods had healed him. The sand paintings show scenes from these stories, and therefore, among their other

PLATE P. 142 functions, also have a mnemotechnical purpose. It is usual to make a new painting each day the ceremony lasts. At the start the sand bed is smoothed down with a weaving batten and on this base are strewn coloaril powder made from varicoloured sandstone, gypsum and charcoal. The medicine man oversees the job, leaving the actual work to his special assistants seconded by other men and youths. Black, white, blue (really a bluish grey), orange and red are the colours used. Sand paintings have either circular or angular forms, and their dimensions can vary a great deal. 'Artistic freedom' is not allowed; rather the intention is to reproduce an old model as closely as possible from memory. This means that particular forms and a particular style are obligatory. Thus men, gods, animals and stars (in so far as these are represented anthropomorphically) bear masks before their faces. The figures can be shown in profile as well as frontally. Because they are made up of geometric forms—parallelograms, rectangles, circles, triangles, lines and bands—these figures display cubistic tendencies, as is also the case with plants and with symbols of particular phenomena. The whole painting is often surrounded on three sides by a protective boundary line that can take various forms, though it commonly appears as a rainbow. Only the east, which is regarded as the auspicious direction, is open, though it is sometimes protected by small symbols. Within the area thus defined the painting itself is arranged. All the figures are endowed with a wealth of symbolic content, which can only be safely interpreted in the context of the particular painting, since the rules can be broken in certain cases. For example, round heads

Figure of the Sio Hemis kachina. The head-dress or *tableta*, which is topped with cloud symbols, bears stylized plants and flowers. Hopi. *Height 44.8 cm. Staatliches Museum für Völkerkunde, Berlin. Cf. p. 137.*

indicate gods and angular ones goddesses, but not always. The colours have a symbolic value too, for not only do they convey the sex, powers and characteristics of given figures, but also have directional connotations. White usually means east, blue south, yellow west and black north. But for magic reasons black and white can be interchanged, as in the example illustrated. Some 1000 different sand paintings of the Navaho are known, all attached to particular ceremonies. Certain highly sacred ones were made on a hide with pollen and meal. Normally the paintings can be seen in their full beauty for a short time only, for they are soon covered over with a layer of pollen and meal. Then the patient seats himself on the surface so as to absorb the accumulated magical energy and the medical man circles around him. At the end the material is carefully mixed with sand and taken out of the hogan. Despite its short lifetime each painting is executed with minute precision and great sensibility; the results are so effective that they are often judged to be the most beautiful examples anywhere of their kind.

Navaho With the Navaho we have gone outside the bounds of Pueblo culture, though we remain in the Southwest. As far as present knowledge indicates, they were late migrants from the north, who probably came with the Apache only shortly before the discovery of America. It is not certain whether they formed a unit at this time, but it can be proved that over the centuries the Navaho have absorbed various other groups, including some Pueblo Indians. Originally nomadic hunters, they soon took over the practice of agriculture from the neighbouring Pueblo groups (though they were often on bad terms with them) and sheep herding from the Spaniards. Their art can also be traced back to these two sources. Like sand painting, weaving—women's work among the Navaho—must stem from the Pueblo. Typical of Navaho weaving are woollen blankets with a basic pattern of strips among which geometric motifs, often stepped lozenges, appear. Figural representations began in the early twentieth century. Silverwork came from Mexico, probably about 1850, and soon became

Figure of the Hon (bear) kachina. Bear kachinas were very powerful and could heal the sick. They appear in the mixed kachina dances. Painted cottonwood. Third Mesa, Hopi. *Height 20 cm. Staatliches Museum für Völkerkunde, Berlin. Cf. p. 137.*

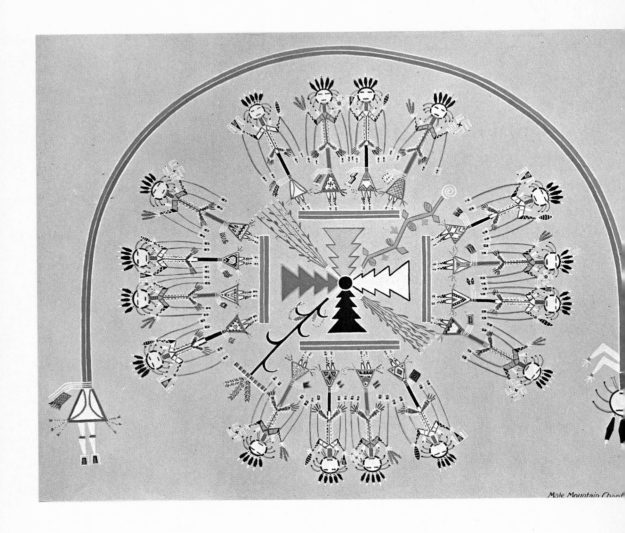

Copy of a sand painting from the ceremony of the 'Male Mountain Chant'. The scene, which is oriented to the cardinal points, is surrounded on three sides by a protective rainbow. Only the 'good' east side is open. In the centre is black water from which radiate four rain clouds in colours appropriate to the direction. For magical reasons the colours for the north (black) and east (white) have been interchanged. Between the clouds we see maize, beans, squash and tobacco growing from the water. On each side are four male mountain gods standing on short rainbows. They were called the 'Reared in the Mountains' and often described as 'bear gods'. They hold rattles, spruce boughs and swastika-shaped whirling baskets. From their joints and elbows hang rain streamers. Navaho. *Original copy, Museum of Navajo Ceremonial Art, Sante Fé, N. M. Cf. p. 138.*

142

a highly specialized industry. The motifs of the pieces cast in sandstone moulds can be derived almost without exception from Spanish or Mexican prototypes.

The linguistically related Apache took no part in this development and their culture and art followed other paths that are more closely connected with the Great Basin and the Plains. Of interest from the artistic standpoint are their coiled baskets, which display black designs against a brownish gold background. Apart from geometric motifs, angular human and animal figures are characteristic. However, the painting of clothing and shields is closely linked to Plains art. The basketry of the Pima and Papago, in which some discern the inheritance of the Hohokam tradition, are of outstanding quality. Complicated geometric designs predominate at the expense of naturalistic motifs. The monochrome pots made by these tribes no longer reveal anything of the old ways. Tradition has proved more lasting among the Yuma and Mohave of the Colorado River area, who may derive from the Patayan culture. Noteworthy are figures and pots with several spouts that are decorated with heads. The geometric designs in reddish brown stand out against a yellowish ground.

Apache and other groups

FIG. 60

FIG. 60 – *Large basket in the coiling technique with black decoration on a light brown ground. Western Apache. Museum für Völkerkunde, Hamburg. Cf. above.*

VII. THE GREAT PLAINS

Geography At one time the vast grasslands of the Great Plains or prairie stretched from the eastern foothills of the Rocky Mountains to the Mississippi and beyond (though in a changed form) and from the Canadian province of Alberta almost as far as the Rio Grande, the southern border dividing the United States from Mexico. Ecologically, one can distinguish two regions—or three if the areas east of the Mississippi are included. In this context, however, only the two west of the great river are really relevant. These are the short-grass steppe with its low rainfall in the west and the eastern tall-grass region that is abundantly watered. It is not surprising that this distinction is also reflected in the indigenous cultures, especially in pre-European times. Outside our immediate concern is the Mississippi Valley itself; it belongs to the cultural region of the Southeast and will be discussed in a later chapter. Although in the last few decades intensive archaeological work has considerably enlarged and modified our knowledge of the settlement of the Great Plains region, the pre-European period can be treated fairly briefly, in as much as no real artistic development or style is detectable. This is not because there was no art, but rather because it was mainly executed in perishable materials not preserved in the archaeological record; this is shown by work from later periods. Without entering into the minor distinctions between particular regions, the discussion that follows presents an outline of the development.

Archaeology We have seen that the Plano culture, as conceived by Krieger, dominated the early period in the Great Plains. Its end is often hard to determine here. While in the High Plains of the west either a break in the sequence of finds or an actual gap existed for the period between 5000 and 2000 B.C., a hunting and collecting culture continued in the eastern part, where the bison seems to have been quite important. About 2000 B.C. this culture appeared in the west as well. During the last 500 years before the beginning of our era a transformation began in the area of the tall grass, stimulated by influence from the east and connected with the Woodland and Hopewell traditions there. Important aspects of this influence are maize and beans, which now appear in the Plains for the first time. Small villages along streams in the alluvial river-bottoms where agriculture could be practised are typical. In the west, however, the hunting and collecting trend persisted. In the ninth century of our era new groups and ideas seem to have penetrated into the eastern prairie, for cultivation of the soil was intensified. An influx from the Mississippi region is likely. Settlements of this type, with agriculture in the valleys and well-organized hunting, stretched as far as the marginal areas of the High Plains. But these outposts were given up shortly before A.D. 1500. At the same time the villages in the east became larger, concentrating along the major watercourses. A new culture developed which reached its climax between 1500 and 1750, and can be clearly followed in tribes of later historical times. At this point the western part of the Great Plains was taken over by bison hunters. The profound changes associated with this led to the formation of the typical Plains culture as it is known to us from the nineteenth century.

The ecological and cultural division into two parts continued long after the arrival of the Europeans in North America. The east, which we must now examine a little more closely, was settled by maize-growing tribes, who belonged to a variety of language families. In the southern part of this region lived tribes of the Caddo family, such as the Pawnee in Nebraska, the Aricara in North Dakota and the Wichita in Kansas —all either originally from the south or strongly influenced from this area. The mass of tribes in the eastern prairie belonged to the Sioux group: Mandan, Hidatsa, Osage, Omaha, Ponca, Oto, Kansa, Iowa and others. They were driven out of the Great Lakes area by Algonquian tribes. Of this last linguistic family, only one tribe, the Cheyenne, lived west of the Mississippi River. But in this context we must also take into account tribes living east of the river, who had settled in the small prairie areas there and who were closely similar in culture to the groups living west of the river. These appear both in the Ohio River area and in the territory of the present states of Illinois and Indiana. They mostly comprise members of the Algonquian family: Sauk and Fox, Miami, Illinois, Kickapoo and Shawnee. They all seem to be late immigrants into a region that belongs archaeologically to the Northeast, driving groups of Sioux over the Mississippi towards the west.

FIG. 61 – *Wooden open-work frame of a dance mirror decorated in chip-carving technique. Sioux, nineteenth century. After Feder, 1964. Cf. p. 153.*

145

Many of these tribes carried on the culture mentioned above in the section on the pre-European period. In some cases it is even possible to correlate archaeological foci with historical tribes and to trace tribal histories back in time. A case in point is the Mandan, whose earliest tangible manifestation seems to be the Thomas Riggs focus of about 1200. Here as in other foci the so-called 'earthen huts' appear quite early, first rectangular, then round; these are typical of the many maize-growing tribes of the eastern prairie, particularly those settled in the area from Nebraska towards the north. The most important building component, a square frame with four vertical posts joined by beams, was slightly sunk into the earth. This frame held the roof timbers, which reached practically to the ground. The roof and walls consisted of several layers of branches, grass and sod, with earth heaped over them. A central fireplace with a rectangular smoke hole over it and a covered entrance are other typical features of this architecture. Also characteristic is the fact that these villages—especially those along the much favoured Missouri River—were almost always fortified with palisades, earthen walls and dry moats, apparently for protection against the Dakota tribes who pressed into the Plains in the seventeenth century. By contrast, the southern tribes of the region lived in open villages made up of domed grass huts, an inheritance from the South-east.

The economic basis of these tribes—often grouped together as the Plains Village Indians—was agriculture in the alluvial river-bottoms, especially along the Missouri and its tributaries. This was on the northern fringe of Indian maize cultivation and consequently special varieties were developed that were suited to the climate with its relatively short growing period; this was a cultural development of the first order. Beans, melons and tobacco were other products of agriculture, which was carried on almost exclusively by women. Their diet was supplemented by hunting, particularly bison, and by fishing from nearby streams.

As implied by the fortified settlements, the villages and tribes had a well-organized system of chieftainship, often with a division of powers between a war and a peace chief, whereby ultimate authority was vested in the latter, while the war chief took charge of military campaigns and in many cases of hunting expeditions as well. Clans were generally present, often ranged into two groups or moieties with ceremonial functions. Apart from belief in an invisible power known by various names, personal visions played an important role. At the age of puberty these were induced through hunger, hardships and

Pipe bowl of catlinite with lead inlay. The inclusion of the naturalistic figures of the man and the bear is quite unusual. Dakota. *Length 17 cm. Linden-Museum, Stuttgart. Cf. p. 153.*

solitude. Those undertaking this regime were rewarded by being shown their personal guardian spirit who, if certain commands were obeyed, would be watchful in time of danger, and the ingredients of the candidate's personal 'medicine', a kind of talisman. Such visions could lead to the conferment of professional status as a shaman and thus the seer might be privileged to join a group of persons endowed with special gifts—the so-called 'medicine-men'. Among the tribes of the southern part of this region this status became increasingly formalized, leading to a greater systematization of religion. Thus, for example, one finds among the Pawnee a genuine sun and star cult with an inherited priesthood, probably created in response to stimuli coming from the Southeast.

While these groups we have been discussing should also be called Plains Indians in a general sense, the mounted bison hunters of the short-grass steppe east of the Rocky Mountains (the so-called High Plains) are considered more typical. Included among them are the Assiniboin, Crow and Teton-Dakota of the Sioux linguistic family, the Gros Ventre, Blackfoot, Arapaho and (later) Cheyenne of the Algonquian family, the Comanche of the Shoshonean family, and the linguistically almost isolated Kiowa, whose nearest relatives are the pueblo-dwelling Tano. Other tribes, chiefly drawn from the originally maize-growing Sioux groups of the eastern Plains, joined these in the course of time, and a part of the Shoshone of the Plateau and some units of the Apache in the south took over many traits of this culture too.

Mounted bison hunters

It has already been mentioned that bison hunters inhabited the short-grass Plains in pre-European times. However, the density of settlement was thin. Only after the introduction of the horse did great changes take place: denser settlement, the formation of a typical Plains Indian culture and extensive alterations in the geographical distribution of the tribes. Although it is still hard to trace the movement of tribes, it is likely that a part of the Sioux, for example, began to push into bison-hunter territory only at this time.

The horse was introduced mainly from the Spanish settlements of the south, where the neighbouring Indian tribes were the first to become acquainted with it. Later, probably during revolts, they carried off animals for their own use. Further raids, particularly by the Apache and Comanche, enabled them to build up their herds. Naturally the first tribes to be mounted sought to secure the superiority they had gained by preventing any further spread of the horse. But open attacks and furtive thefts soon broke this monopoly. Thus the use of the horse spread in a wave-like pattern over the Great Plains from the south, while contributions from the French and English territories in the East and Northeast remained minor. One of the most important lines of transmission ran through the Great Basin and the Plateau region within the Rocky Mountains. Here the Shoshone were on horseback at the latest by 1690, becoming the lords of the north-western Plains. The Palouse in southern Washington bred a special race of horses that still exists today, the Appalousians. In north-eastern Oregon the Cayuse were horse traders par excellence, giving their name to the Indian horse as a general epithet. But no sooner was dominance achieved than it melted away, as the example of the Shoshone demonstrates: towards the middle of the eighteenth century they were driven

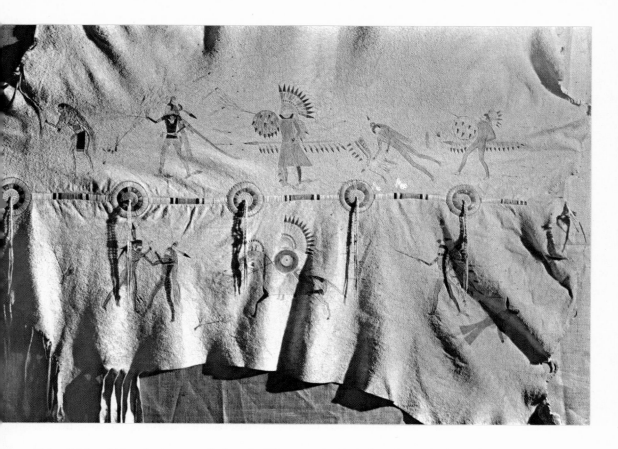

Painted bison-hide robe in naturalistic style. The central strip is done in porcupine-quill work. The robe was painted by the Mandan chief Matotope and shows some of his achievements, especially his victories over other chiefs. Mandan, mid-nineteenth century. *Size 172 × 212 cm. Linden-Museum, Stuttgart. Cf. p. 154.*

back into their old homeland—after the neighbouring Blackfoot had acquired not only horses, but also guns from Canadian traders. The Blackfoot then became the lords of the north-western Plains, waging an unceasing struggle with other tribes to defend their position. But the Shoshone had become so fully assimilated to the Plains Indian way of life that they could hardly do without bison hunting. Despite constant threats from the Blackfoot, hunting expeditions were sent into the western prairie and survival through the winter depended on

149

them. By 1770 at the latest there was no tribe in the western Plains that was not mounted. In this way the Plains culture of the mounted bison hunters developed, which led to a new climax of Indian life, though this lasted only about a century during which time it was strongly impregnated by European trade goods and partly dependent on them. But for Europeans today these mounted tribes provide the typical picture of the North American Indians. The basis of this culture was bison hunting. The welfare of the tribe depended on the result of the seasonal hunt and thus it is not surprising that it was strictly regulated and surrounded with many ceremonies. This was a community hunt carried out either by the whole tribe or by a sizeable sub-group. There was a kind of police force, consisting mainly of members of the 'dog society', to enforce strong laws against anyone who might try to start hunting too soon or on his own and thus frighten away the animals. Different customs existed among the several tribes for distributing the game, which might either be shared out or awarded to the man who had actually made the kill. All the meat that was not consumed immediately was cut into thin strips and dried in the sun. Later it was reduced to powder, mixed with dried and mashed berries, and covered over with fat and marrow. This pemmican, as the preparation was called, was kept in big leather bags known as parfleches. The pemmican helped the Indians to get through the times when no bison were hunted, particularly the winter months. In this season the tribe broke up into small groups which would be better able to feed themselves by hunting small animals. Then in spring they came together once more to prepare for bison hunting.

It was not only the meat of the bison that was used by these Indians, but other parts were exploited as well, such as the bones, tendons and particularly the hide, which the women worked into leather. From this material they made clothing and shoes (mocassins), shields and cradle-boards, saddles and bridles. They also produced pouches, buckets and bags that served to replace pottery which had formerly been used to some extent. Leather was particularly important for the covering of the tepee, the characteristic conical tent. At first small and used only in hunting expeditions, the tent became larger and more spacious with the appearance of the horse, so that it replaced all other forms of dwelling. Previously only dogs were available to transport the supports and tent covers with the help of a kind of sledge (the travois), but horses took their place and these could drag much heavier weights with the travois.

FIG. 62 – *Bison-leather shield with polychrome painting. Linked to activities of the bison society. Northern Blackfoot. After Wissler, 1912. Cf. p. 158.*

The village was laid out around three-quarters of a circle, open to the east, and each sub-group had its own fixed and hereditary place. Sacred tents and council tents were found within the circle, though not always in the centre. Sub-groups, sometimes exogamous clans and sometimes less formal units, consisted of one or more 'chiefs' with their following. The chiefs, who acquired their office either through inheritance or through election, made up the council of the tribe or a part of it; they chose among themselves one or more leaders who had specific functions but who could not rule arbitrarily. It is not surprising that these customs varied from tribe to tribe, though in some instances differences were slight. Similarly the tribal divisions could

then choose one or more tribal chiefs, as with the Crow. In other cases, although common membership in a tribe was recognized, a single overall authority was lacking, as with the Blackfoot and the Sioux-speaking Dakota. Finally, the voluntary associations and military societies must be mentioned: these were assigned certain specified tasks, as mentioned in connexion with bison hunts. Entrance procedures, eligibility and ceremonies are so varied that it is impossible to discuss them here.

In religion the mounted bison hunters share many common features with the Plains Village culture. In fact much of the hunters' religion must derive from the village dwellers or at least from a common source. But certain aspects, such as the evocation of protective spirits through visions, received more stress. The 'sacred bundle', which was the property of a tribe, division, society or individual, was also more prominent among bison hunters. This custom reached its apogee among the Pawnee. Here the close link with maize growing was expressed by the fact that the most essential part of the bundle was a cob of maize, while among many bison-hunting tribes the place of honour belonged to a sacred pipe.

ART So far we have not dealt specifically with the art of either of the two groups who inhabited the Great Plains. This reservation was intentional, for nowhere else are the connexions as close as in this region, so that the art can best be treated *en bloc*. Of course differences do exist, but these are significant more for individual tribes than for the two main divisions of this vast cultural region. In any case the differences are so minor that they can safely be ignored here.

It is best to begin with the lesser categories of art. Among these are *Carving* incised decorations on tools and other objects of daily use made of bone; these patterns are mostly geometric. Closely related are the carvings in and on wood used to adorn weapons and other objects. Decorative frames for dance mirrors ornamented in chip-carving FIG. 61 technique seem to have been especially popular among the Sioux tribes. Only one form of sculpture appeared among the Plains Indians: pipe bowls made of catlinite. This Minnesota stone is very soft when PLATE P. 147 broken, so that it is often spoken of as 'pipe clay', but it soon hardens on being exposed to the air. This facilitated working in various shapes that were developed by individual tribes. But simple types for everyday use were in the majority. When sculptural ornaments were present, they were realistically handled, and depicted men and animals. Certain similarities with the pipes of the East are evident, though the links have not yet been clarified. This art form was especially cultivated among the Dakota, who held the territory in which the pipestone quarries lay and who spread their products among their neighbours. They may have originated the custom of adorning pipe bowls with lead or pewter inlay. How far European influence was operative here cannot be determined.

While carving can be regarded as a simple, almost rudimentary art *Painting* and pottery and weaving were either entirely lacking, or in the case

FIG. 64 – *Hunting pouch with porcupine-quill embroidery. Shawnee. Linden-Museum, Stuttgart. Cf. p. 158.*

153

of eastern pottery showed forms with scarcely any ornamentation, another category of Plains art reached a height unequalled elsewhere in North America: the embellishment of leather objects with painting and embroidery. Stylistically we can distinguish a naturalistic and a geometric trend; the former type appears only in painting, the latter in both media.

Turning first to the naturalistic style, the finest work appears on the so-called bison robes. These are skins that are worn with the smooth side against the body in summer and the reverse in winter. The smooth side of these robes was frequently painted, above all with human figures, animals and objects, supplemented by a series of symbols. The process of making them was as follows: the outlines of the figures intended were first pressed or embossed into the leather with a blunt tool. Then the artist applied earth or vegetable colours, filling the areas defined by the lines with the aid of a brush made of a frayed piece of wood. The imagery of the paintings, which at first appears confused, becomes comprehensible as soon as one learns something of the meaning, which is closely connected with the art of war as practised by the Plains Indians. The paintings on the robes recount the deeds of the owner-wearer—his special feats, his battles and, if of importance, the gifts he has distributed. Thus they amounted to public documents subject to constant inspection so that it was impossible to get by with fictional exploits. At the same time the paintings had a narrative value, serving as an aid to memory. In this sense they recall pictographs, a term that is sometimes applied to them, though not entirely correctly. A kindred phenomenon is that of the so-called 'winter counts' of the Sioux, especially the Dakota, in which the most important events of the year were described, so that they took on the qualities of a chronicle. How far the European example made itself felt here is uncertain. But there is evidence that figure painting on leather is quite old, possibly even pre-European. This indicates that the robes were often painted by the owner himself. Consequently the execution and quality of the paintings are quite variable. Some reach

PLATE P. 149 an astonishing degree of development, as in the surviving robes of the Mandan chief Matotope. Despite these differences, which are also conditioned by tribal traditions, certain general features can be identified that recur in most or all of the paintings. Basic to their aesthetic is the fact that perspective is entirely absent, as are such details of landscape setting as mountains or trees. The individual scenes that make up the paintings—a single scene covering the whole hide is unusual—are often arranged in strips one above the other. Oddly

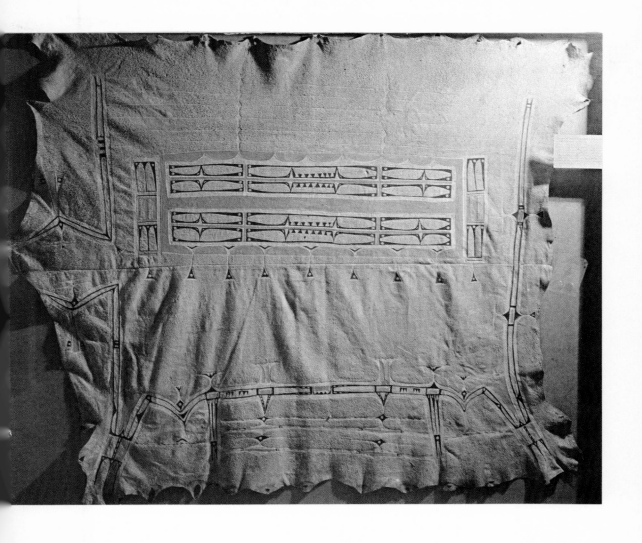

Painted bison-hide robe. The geometrical ornament in the centre belongs to the class of 'earth symbols'. Dakota, nineteenth century. *Size 158 × 198 cm. Linden-Museum, Stuttgart. Cf. p. 158.*

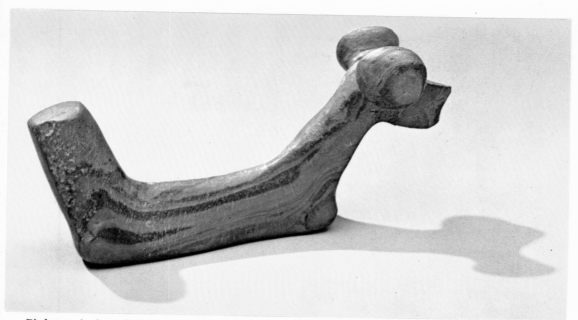

Birdstone in bounded slate. Scholars believe that these objects served as counterweights for spear-throwers, but the interpretation is still rather uncertain. Because of the emphasis on the eyes this piece must be dated in the Late Archaic period. Found in Ontario. *Royal Ontario Museum, Toronto.* *Cf. p. 163.*

enough the native animals, particularly the bison, are better drawn than the men and horses. The latter are often quite stiff and the human figures, which recall those of children's paintings, can often be described as 'primitive'. But it may be that the effects of a certain tendency towards abstraction are evident here. Real profile views are rare and if present probably reflect European influence. The pictorial problem of the horse and rider was rarely solved, for the legs of the rider are often omitted, or else both legs were shown on the flank visible to the observer. It is, however, quite possible that the concept of the X-ray view may have been operative here. Its effect may be noted in other scenes where the body of a man is shown beneath his

Leather tobacco pouch decorated with glass-bead embroidery. The central motif of four stylized eagles is rather uncommon in this medium. Dakota. *Length 34 cm. Staatliches Museum für Völkerkunde, Berlin.* *Cf. p. 160.*

clothing and shield. Protective spirits and visions are also depicted in naturalistic fashion on robes. Paintings similar to those described appear not only on robes, but also on the poncho-like over-garments of the men, on tents, and on drums and shields, as well as their coverings. Shield coverings are often characterized by a particular style that is more abstract and stylized. This shift may be explained by the difference in context, for shields and their coverings are almost exclusively painted with representations of visions or with images of protective spirits.

Geometric motifs appear on bison-hide robes. They comprise two groups of patterns that can be described as solar and celestial symbols on one hand and earth symbols on the other. The first group, which was supposed to be worn by men only, consists of several concentric circles. Because of the stylized feathers introduced, these patterns can sometimes be understood as a semi-abstract rendering of a feather cap. While the possibility of a valid interpretation exists here, this is lacking for the often very complicated 'earth motif', which is restricted to women's robes. It is a striking fact that though this motif occurs among very different tribes, it always remains quite stable in form. Other geometric motifs, such as feathers, 'puberty symbols' and single strips, occur on robes, but are rather infrequent. The painted decoration of the parfleches is entirely geometric, as is that of the cylindrical leather containers for feather caps and of the rectangular leather pillows. Lozenges and rectangles are important motifs here. The patterns of embroidery are almost always geometric and stylized images of men and animals appear only rarely. Technically speaking, the term 'embroidery' is a misnomer, for appliqué work is invariably the technique here and the decorative material is not carried through on to the back. But the expression has been used for so long that it would be difficult to change it. The oldest and best known of these methods of 'embroidery' is that which uses the quills of the tree porcupine *(erithizon dorsatus)*. Since the origins of this technique lie in the Northeast they will be discussed further in that context. Quill work must have been introduced into the Great Plains through the migration of certain tribes, particularly those of the Sioux group. It is surprising that the technique should have been so highly developed here, for the quills had to be specially imported from the forest habitat of the tree porcupine. The hollow quills were coloured, split apart and flattened. Then they were sewn invisibly with sinew on leather. A continuous row could be made by interlocking many of the rather short quills. The number of methods used in sewing them is so large that they cannot be discussed separately here. But it should be noted that the broader strips were first woven completely in a special technique and then attached to the leather. The patterns too are very numerous and often vary from tribe to tribe, so that individual pieces can be classified according to their tribe of origin. Studies of the typical Plains types of mocassins with hard leather soles have shown that both in form and motif a number of categories can be distinguished. There are eight different arrangements, grouped in two main classes: those partly open on top and those completely covered. Besides these two, other combinations can be distinguished which can, however, be traced back to the main layouts. Both classes comprise the following schemes: decorated border, decorated border with centre strip and decorated border with two centre strips. In addition, some mocassins are fully decorated without distinguishable borders or strips and still others have only a short ornamental strip. A ninth type has a decoration in a small, often U-shaped centre field. The reason for saying that only eight different arrangements can be distinguished is that the partly open type with a decorated border exists only with the last-mentioned (ninth) layout. Six kinds of basic motifs are employed. The range of variation among these motifs—step pyramid, simple pyramid, cross, lozenge, 'earth motif' and chevron—is considerable and through various combinations becomes almost limitless. We cannot attempt to summarize the various studies that have been made on the diffusion of these arrangements and motifs. Suffice it to say that the more complicated motifs seem to have developed in recent times, when they became less widespread than the simpler ones. Characteristic of all these products (and probably reflecting the nature of the material) is the fact that hard, angular patterns are preferred, often with sharply contrasting colours. The usual background is white.

Quill work was employed to decorate not only mocassins and such other leather goods as clothing, pouches, cradle-boards and quivers, but also objects in wood, particularly the long, oval-sectioned stems of tobacco-pipes, as well as knife handles and other pieces. After the appearance of the first European traders, quills were partly replaced by glass beads, though porcupine quill work persisted and is still

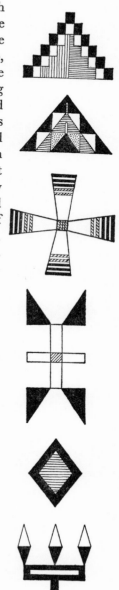

FIG. 65 – *Chief motifs of mocassin decoration in porcupine-quill and bead embroidery in the Plains. From top to bottom: step pyramid, simple pyramid, cross, angle pattern, lozenge, 'earth motif'. After Wissler, 1927. Cf. above.*

practised here and there today. Typical of the bead work of the Plains tribes is the so-called 'lazy stitch', in which several beads are strung on the thread between each attachment to the base. The hard, geometric patterns that we have already encountered in quill work continued, PLATE P. 156 despite the new possibilities offered by glass beads. However, some new colours were introduced. Stylized living forms are rare in these techniques, though highly abstract birds are not infrequent. The leather objects mentioned above continued to be decorated as well as the jackets and waistcoats of European cut which were now introduced.

VIII. THE NORTHEAST

Geography

The Southwest, California and the Northwest Coast are fairly well defined areas. In the Plains it was already more difficult to fix the boundaries, but this was an easy task in comparison with that posed by the region now to be discussed, the Northeast. Only one boundary can be drawn with certainty—the Atlantic Ocean on the east. The other boundaries all represent a compromise, for cultural interchange with neighbouring regions was so intense that lines of separation were sometimes effaced altogether. Thus on the southern border, which coincides with that of the present states of Virginia and Kentucky, a continuous forward and backward movement and an overlapping of cultural traits can be discerned that suggests the possibility of treating the Northeast and the Southeast as a single unit. The western border also, which can be fixed at the Mississippi River, was subject to considerable oscillation, as the preceding chapter has shown. In the north the region stretches as far as the Hudson Bay, where it meets the Eskimo area.

Another distinguishing quality of the Northeast is that geographically it is definitely not a homogeneous region with similar environmental conditions throughout. Instead, we find a kaleidoscopic range of ecological units stretching from the coastal plain on the Atlantic across the Alleghenies and their foothills to the alluvial river-bottoms of the Mississippi and the Ohio Valleys, and from the rocky coasts of Newfoundland to the banks of the Great Lakes. The vegetation undergoes considerable change not only because of different surface conditions, but also because of the climate, which ranges from near tundra in the north to oak forests in the south. It is significant that the northern limits of Indian cultivation lie within this region. Various ways of life were open to the early inhabitants of the Northeast and it is not surprising that differences should soon appear and be ever more strongly accentuated.

In the beginning the Northeast was occupied by groups characterized by the use of channelled projectile points, which they may have employed to hunt large diluvial animals. But it is more likely that collecting, fishing and hunting of small game provided the main sources of food supply. About 10,000 B.C. these Indians lived on the edge of the glacial

ARCHAEOLOGY

FIG. 66 – *Stone slab with carved pattern depicting a bird of prey. Adena culture, Ohio. After Griffin, 1952. Cf. p. 168.*

ice pack that at this time lay just north of Chicago. Here in the area of the Great Lakes vast changes took place in the following millennia affecting the surface picture: fed by the retreating and advancing ice masses, lakes appeared and disappeared, and the edge of forests moved north and south correspondingly. Thus ice and water, tundra and forests—whether deciduous or evergreen—alternated, creating new conditions to which men had to adjust, until about 500 B.C., when approximately the present situation was reached.

After 7000 B.C. the makers of the channelled projectile points disappeared. Since the last advance of ice ended at this time it may be correct to assume that these groups who had specialized in hunting along the edge of the ice followed it northwards. In their place there appear in the Great Lakes district other units, which are grouped under the term Aqua-Plano and which seem to be related to the Plano tradition of the Plains. The Aqua-Plano people were hunters, fishers and collectors who lived in temporary camps along the banks of the lakes and streams. About 4500 B.C. they yielded to other groups and disappeared from our ken. At this time the Indian groups known collectively under the term 'Early Archaic' lived elsewhere in the Northeast. Their rough-surfaced stone tools show that they were still simple game hunters. This population, which spread towards the Great Lakes, provided the basis out of which developed many of the specialized groups of later times.

Late Archaic period The following 'Late Archaic' period, which lasts until about 1000 B.C., has both coastal and forest traditions. They include numerous complexes and phases that pose problems of correlation, though, with one exception, their repertory of forms is quite homogeneous. Besides blades, points and other chipped instruments there now appear ground stone tools, especially for working wood—gouges, adzes and celts. The northern part also produced ground slate objects that recall Eskimo work. That the spear-thrower was used is proved by a number of ground stone objects which must have served as counter-

weights for this weapon. Because of the craftsmen's preference for fine-veined stones and for balanced and strict forms, these 'banner stones' can be appreciated as abstract works of art. Although we know the use here, this is not the case with other objects, such as the 'stone feathers' and the 'birdstones'. The latter occur only towards the end of the period and are already quite abstract in appearance. Although Early Archaic examples have the eyes strongly emphasized, they almost disappear in the later pieces. Whether these objects made of slate or veined stone are also connected with spear-throwers is highly doubtful. Finally we must mention bowls made of soapstone, which are particularly common in the coastal tradition.

Although no settlements from this period are known, a certain degree of sedentary life must be assumed together with a more intensive exploitation of the possibilities offered by the environment. Burials took the most varied forms and their diversity mirrors numerous local and regional developments. About 1500 B.C. a custom began to spread that was seemingly independent of local variations and preferences; this can be described as a special ritual for the dead. It introduced a cultural development, traceable up to the inception of the European period, in which the dead were of great importance. The first indications of this cult of the dead are termed the 'Red Ochre complex' because of the characteristic scattering of powdered ochre over open graves.

Old Copper culture

In virtue of its importance for later developments, another culture of this period deserves special attention. This is the Old Copper culture in the region of the Great Lakes with a central focus west of Lake Michigan. Their representatives collected copper on Isle Royale and on the Keeweenaw peninsula, where it appears on or near the surface in pure form, and fashioned ornaments and tools from it by cold hammering and tempering. Smelting and casting were unknown and remained so until the arrival of the Europeans. The extensive repertory

FIG. 68 – *End of a spatulate object of bone with engraved bird figure. The treatment of the curved lines is characteristic of the bone carvings of the Hopewell culture. Found at the Turner Group, Little Miami Valley, Ohio. After Willoughby, 1917. Cf. p. 171.*

of copper objects includes spear points with shaft sockets of thorns for attachment, knives, adzes, celts, awls, needles and fish hooks. Ornaments included spherical or elongated beads strung for necklaces, pendants and bracelets. Some of these objects seem to resemble in shape early European pieces. This has suggested the hypothesis of direct migration and transmission from the Old World. However, two facts speak against this: (1) Other aspects of the Old Copper culture are not essentially different from those of other cultures of the region during this period. Like their neighbours, the Old Copper people were collectors and hunters, who also used the readily accessible copper deposits only because they were convenient. Obviously a brisk trade grew up and their products were diffused as far as New York and Manitoba. (2) It appears that Old Copper culture is a good deal earlier than the European Bronze Age. Unfortunately not all dates have yet been firmly established. It can be safely assumed, however, that this culture was already in existence before 3000 B.C. and is thus older than the Bronze Age, even in the Mediterranean basin, and approximately contemporary with the earliest copper objects of this area. Isolated carbon 14 findings even suggest that the beginnings of this culture go back to about 5000 B.C. If so, this may be the earliest metal-working culture in the world, a fact that is very little known. In any case, however, it can be affirmed that the Old Copper culture arose independently and that it represents one of the earliest copper cultures in human history known to us.

This culture faded out about 1500 B.C. Since a gradual shift towards the north was already in progress earlier, we may perhaps assume that this occurred in response to the gradual northward shift of a specialized animal and plant world upon which these people were dependent. A gradual increase in warmth would have displaced the Indians' normal environment towards the Pole. Thus eventually their main territory would no longer include the district of the copper deposits and metal production would consequently cease. But the tradition of copper working remained, carried on either by the groups that stayed behind or by new units, for the above-mentioned Red Ochre complex included copper objects, as did the Glacial Kame burial complex, *Burial ceremonialism* which is also part of early burial ceremonialism. In this complex the dead were interred in a flexed position in natural mounds. Typical grave goods are sole-shaped gorgets made of shell, often ornamented with simple incisions. Copper was used for ornaments and tools (awls, adzes, needles). Arrow points were chipped, while other tools were ground and polished, such as the 'birdstones', adzes and tubular

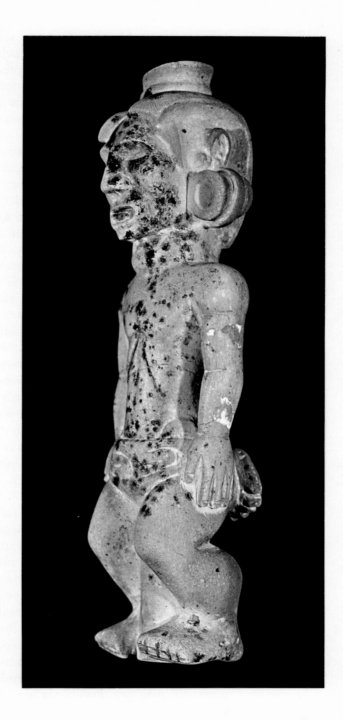

Stone smoking tube in the form
of a dancing man. This famous
piece is notable not only for the
information it gives on dress at
the time of its manufacture, but
also because it represents an
artistic peak of the Adena culture. The mouthpiece is attached
to the head and the tobacco
bowl lies between the feet. Adena
culture. Found at Adena Mound,
Ross County, Ohio. *Length 19.8
cm. Ohio State Museum, Columbus.
Cf. p. 168.*

tobacco-pipes. Connexions with the cult of the dead are clearly indicated by the use of powdered ochre in many cases.

Apart from burial customs, the spread of burial ceremonialism over large parts of the Northeast did not change the existing cultures in any essential way. The motive force directing this diffusion is unclear, but it may have been a new religion. The cult not only spread within the bounds of the forest tradition where it originated, but appeared on the coast as well, as in the Orient complex on Long Island Sound. Powdered ochre occurred here again, but either with cremations or with secondary burials. The absence of copper objects and the use of soapstone bowls are further evidence that the idea of burial ceremonialism was simply grafted on to the existing culture complexes. Between 1500 and 500 B.C. the Late Archaic period merged gradually and imperceptibly into the Early Woodland period, which in fact represents simply an advanced archaic stage with the addition of pottery, a somewhat artificial basis of distinction. Life continued to flourish in all its previous forms, except that ceramic vessels took the place of containers in other materials. Nonetheless, some scholars persist in attributing this change to influences or even actual migrations from Asia or Meso-America. But no proof of this has been forthcoming. The idea of pottery may have come from elsewhere, but forms and decoration showed local characteristics at a very early date. Decoration by impressions of cords and coarse textiles in the wet clay gave the region's products a distinctive appearance and anticipated the later emphasis on plastic decorations.

Adena The most important development of this period and one of the high points of the Northeast was the Adena culture in the middle Ohio Valley, which lasted approximately from 800 B.C. to A.D. 200. Here large-scale burial mounds first appeared—grouped in precincts surrounded by earth walls with palisades and entrances. Since no house foundations have yet been found inside the walls, these precincts were obviously not settlements but holy places. Walled precincts of this type are characteristic of the apogee of the Adena culture, which in its beginnings shows only small isolated mounds, as do other contemporary complexes. The apogee, which starts shortly before the beginning of our era, will be treated in what follows. Houses were round in plan and wider above than below; the pointed roof and wattle walls were covered with mats. Each settlement comprised only a few of these houses and there were no larger concentrations. This may be due to economic requirements; collecting and hunting were still primary. Possibly a kind of gardening was practised with

Stone platform pipe. The bowl is shaped naturalistically in the form of a bear. Hopewell culture. Found at Tremper Mound, Scioto County, Ohio. *Length 8.85 cm. Height of bear 4.4 cm. Ohio State Museum, Columbus. Cf. p. 172.*

plants of Meso-American origin such as maize, pumpkins and melons, together with such local specialities as sunflowers and tobacco. Gardening of this kind (of which we are not even certain yet) may have guaranteed a more regular food supply, but was never more than a supplementary source. One should not assume, however, that these plants were introduced directly by immigrants from the south. More likely is a slow infiltration via the Gilmore corridor in Texas. Burial ceremonialism, too, is indigenous rather than imported, deriving from such forerunners as Glacial Kame and Red Ochre. During the apogee of the Adena culture the dead were laid in wooden tomb chambers in the mounds, which rose higher with each new burial. Numerous objects, often quite valuable, were buried with the dead, who appear to have belonged to an elevated social class. For this reason we are well informed about the crafts of this period. These rich tombs show that because of the extensive use of wild plants—primarily acorns, then walnuts, hickory nuts and other fruits and seeds—there was enough surplus to maintain specialized craftsmen.

Many objects of daily use in the Adena culture derive from prototypes from older phases. Some things—adzes and arrow-heads of stone, awls and adzes of copper—remained unchanged. The use of copper for personal ornaments increased; beads, gorgets, bracelets and finger rings were now made in this material. Pottery was relatively unimportant: the flat-bottomed vessels are usually undecorated and only one type shows incised geometric patterns. But stone work flourished.

PLATE P. 165 Of this work, one pipe is outstanding not only in Adena but also in all the art of the Northeast. Anthropomorphically conceived, it represents a dancer. This appears to be an isolated piece, however, since most pipes continue the tradition of the smoking tubes that were only rarely elaborated in animal or human form, never reaching the high level of the 'dancer pipe'.

FIG. 66 Another special feature are the slate tablets—occasionally these are of clay instead—with deeply incised decorations. The leading motif is the head or whole figure of a bird of prey. The decorations are so curvilinear that the effect is quite baroque. In many cases the motifs are hard to recognize. The purpose of these tablets has not yet been determined.

It is understandable that such a high level of development exercised an influence on neighbouring areas, for many cultures of the Northeast continued to live under modified 'Archaic' conditions. It is not yet clear whether influences of this kind—like those found in the Delaware Valley and Chesapeake Bay, but also in the Southeast—were due to trade or migration. It is certain that Adena also influenced the development of another climax of the Northeast, the Hopewell culture with its centre in the Ohio-Illinois region.

Pottery vessel with zoned decoration. The main motif in the form of a bird of prey was demarcated with shallow grooves and left smooth, while the background was roughened with a rocker stamp. Richly decorated vessels of this type were chiefly used for ceremonial purposes. Hopewell culture. Found at Mound Group City, Ross County, Ohio. *Height 15.4 cm. Ohio State Museum, Columbus. Cf. p. 171.*

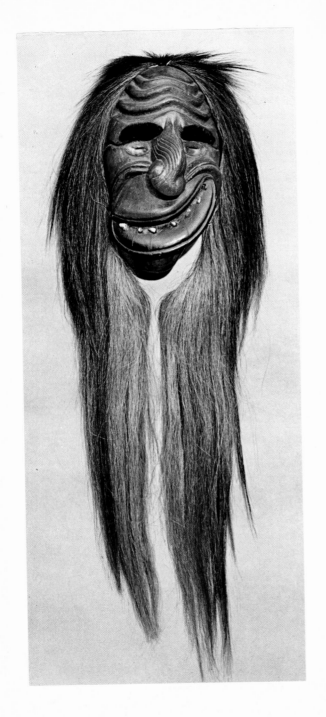

Mask of the 'False-Face society'. This special mask type is called 'crooked mouth'. Painted poplar wood with inlaid brass eyes, deer teeth and horse hair. Iroquois, nineteenth century. *Height 31 cm. Royal Ontario Museum, Toronto. Cf. p. 177.*

Hopewell seems to have developed about 300 B.C. in the Illinois
Valley from an Early Woodland complex. Illinois continued to be a
focus of this culture, serving as a point of departure for diffusion towards the Great Lakes area and the Missouri, where the inhabitants
were strongly influenced by Hopewell. But the culture seems to have
reached its zenith in the Ohio Valley, where it appeared about 100
B.C. The Adena culture was gradually superseded, though it lived
on in Kentucky. Adena seems to have given the Ohio Hopewell a
push towards the special development that made it the artistic climax
of the Northeast in pre-Columbian times. This region, too, emitted
influences, but they are much more diffuse than those from Illinois;
we will meet them again in the Southeast.

Hopewell represents a culmination of burial ceremonialism in the
western part of the Northeast. As in Adena the burial precincts were
surrounded by earth walls and the tombs, surmounted by regular artificial hills, were carefully lined with wooden planks or bark. Apart
from the body, buried in extended position, of the dead or his ashes,
they held a great variety of fine grave goods. Social differences are
implied by the degree of luxury. As in Adena the economic basis for
this development was still a mixture of collecting and agriculture,
though the importance of maize seems to have increased.

It would take too long to enumerate all the objects produced by the
Hopewell culture. Many of them date back to the 'Archaic' period—
stone adzes and knives, copper axes and awls, as well as birdstones.
Some we have already met in the Adena culture. Other things, such
as work in silver and meteoric iron, are new. Pottery followed the
lines established earlier: decoration continued to be plastic and was
executed with rocker stamps, cord impressions and incisions. A special
type, which probably had a ceremonial function, was 'zoned'—that is, PLATE P. 169
the craftsman produced his patterns by separating smooth and roughened patches with grooved lines which emphasized the pattern.
A common motif was the bird of prey, known from other media as
well. It appears either as a whole or in part—the head or claws—on
copper and mica objects made to adorn clothing or used as grave goods.
From these materials the 'Hopewellians' cut fish, human figures,
antlers, teeth, stylized snake heads and curvilinear geometric orna- FIG. 67
ments. Like copper and mica they imported for their burial ceremonialism other material from remote areas, including conch shells from
the Gulf Coast and obsidian from the Black Hills and Yellowstone.
An outstanding achievement in two-dimensional surface ornamen- FIG. 68
tation is represented by the decorated bone objects, in which geometric

and naturalistic themes are incised in precise curvilinear patterns. However, the mastery of the Hopewell craftsmen was not limited to flat patterns, but extended to three-dimensional objects as well. This is already demonstrated by the small hand-shaped clay figures that have been found at several sites. But all other works were overshadowed by the characteristic platform pipes of stone, rarely of clay, which can be considered the highest artistic achievement of the Hopewell culture and of the Northeast as a whole. Although many of them have only a simple cylinder in the centre of the gently curved platform, there are hundreds of others in which the pipe bowl shows human, or

PLATE P. 167 more commonly animal forms. Hawks, owls, ducks, bears, beavers, otters, wildcats and frogs are depicted with a naturalism rarely found in ancient America, which makes these pieces coveted collectors' items. These figures show certain similarities to hollow statuettes made of stone and horn that are of uncertain significance.

Hopewell represents one of the artistic peaks of North America, in as much as its craftsmen knew how to combine detailed observation of nature with abstraction and with a related category of more *mouvementé* geometric design. An unusual variety of materials and forms distinguishes this culture, which is not yet widely enough known or appreciated and whose products can successfully compete with the best that was being done in many parts of the world at this time. Beside Hopewell, the other contemporary cultures of the North and Northeast, which have left few objects of artistic quality, fade into insignificance.

Late period Possibly due to a decline in climatic conditions, the once powerful Hopewell culture disappeared about A.D. 500, giving way to a number of successor cultures; none approached Hopewell in artistic achieve-

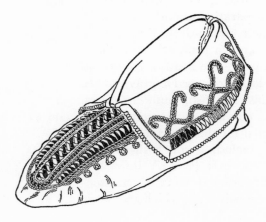

FIG. 69 – *Leather mocassin decorated with porcupine-quill embroidery, cloth and glass beads. A modified double-curve motif is clearly recognizable on the side. Iroquois. Museum für Völkerkunde, Hamburg. Cf. p. 179.*

Cloth collar richly embroidered with glass beads. Although the material and the central flower pattern is one of European origin, the double-curve motifs distributed along the border show the persistence of a strong Indian quality. Penobscot, about 1890. *Length 57 cm.; width 53 cm. The University Museum, Philadelphia, Pa. Cf. p. 179.*

ment. Here and there burial mounds were still built, but they are usually small and lack precinct walls. An exception is the Effigy Mound culture (Wisconsin; A.D. 800–1300), so termed because of the huge mounds that commonly take the form of animals. But no special art products distinguish this culture, apart from occasional 'elbow pipes' in clay, the basic form of which is widely diffused. For some reason, about A.D. 500 the Northeast ceased to be a cultural centre. While it had, until then, strongly influenced the Southeast, the stream of goods, ideas and men now moved in the opposite direction. This is particularly noticeable after about A.D. 900 with the Middle Mississippi tradition stemming from the Southeast. With their advanced maize-growing techniques and fortified villages, these Indians pushed into the old Hopewell territory and took possession of the valleys they needed. Aztalan in Wisconsin, Cahokia near St. Louis and Fort Ancient in the Ohio Valley all attest to this expansion. Other groups of the Northeast took over many features of this culture, which will be discussed in the following chapter. This process may have contributed to the fact that by A.D. 1600 all the cultures south of the St. Lawrence River had reached a large measure of uniformity, with similar agricultural practices, similar houses and similar tools. Major differences, such as those found during the Hopewell period, were lacking.

Something must be said of the coastal tradition, which has been largely neglected in the preceding pages. This continued the whole time, participating marginally in the interior development. Divided into many phases and complexes, it produced some objects of the minor arts here and there; among these the horn carvings are worth noting. But the complicated general picture forbids detailed discussion. In any case these cultures are primarily of interest to the specialist.

ETHNOLOGY
Iroquois

When the Europeans arrived, Indians of three language groups occupied the Northeast: Iroquois, Algonquians and Sioux. These larger groupings were split up into small, even minuscule units, of which only a few can be mentioned here. Sometimes they joined together to form leagues, the Iroquois Confederation, which called itself the Hodinonhsioni, the 'People of the Long House', being the most important. Originally comprising five tribes (Onondaga, Cayuga,

Painted coat of European cut. The decoration is dominated by the double-curve motif widely diffused in the Northeast. Naskapi. *Length 109 cm. Museum of the American Indian, Heye Foundation, New York, N. Y. Cf. p. 179.*

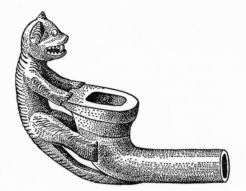

FIG. 70 – *Clay pipe bowl with the figure of a bear. Iroquois, seventeenth century. National-museet, Copenhagen. Cf. p. 181.*

Mohawk, Oneida and Seneca), in 1722 the league enrolled another Iroquois group, the Tuscarora, who had migrated from North Carolina. The Confederation was largely limited to the tribes of Iroquoian language who lived south-east of Lake Ontario, while a whole series of linguistic kin in the Great Lakes area, including the Huron, Erie and Neutral Indians, were left outside. But the material culture of all these northern tribes was so homogeneous that members of the Confederation can serve as examples for the rest.

The Iroquois were farmers who cultivated maize, beans, pumpkins, sunflowers and tobacco; they supplemented their diet by gathering wild plants, hunting and fishing. Their villages were situated in a defensive position on hill-tops and fortified with one or more palisades and sometimes with earth walls as well. Archaeology shows that this type was already found in pre-European times. But under European influence settlements greatly increased in size until by the beginning of the eighteenth century some of them held over a thousand people. Although the houses grouped together in such towns were of different sizes, accommodating one or several families, the building scheme was always the same: a long rectangle with vertical walls and a roof of flattened curvilinear section. The roof was later heightened so as to become almost a barrel vault. Like the walls, the roof had a bark sheathing. The individual tribes were organized into matrilinear, matrilocal clans and the Confederation was governed by fifty sachems, forming the Great Council. Their titles (like other dignities) were inherited in the female line. The religion of the Iroquois was originally dualistic and consequently the clans were grouped into two phratries. But thanks largely to the work of the prophet Handsome Lake in the early nineteenth century this dualism was modified in favour of the 'good' side, which acquired the status of an elevated deity. For us the most interesting aspect of Iroquois religion is the secret societies, especially the 'False-Face' groups, whose members still don masks on special occasions. In the observance of certain rituals involving the offering of tobacco these masks were—and are—carved into the trunk of a living tree to be separated only after completion. The various types of masks sometimes take grotesque forms. They are painted and occasionally decked out with corn husks or horse hair. They represent spirits with the power to heal sickness, the main concern of the False-Face society. Corn-husk masks produced by another of these societies are among the most widespread products of Iroquois art. Before continuing our study of Iroquois objects, however, we must turn briefly to other tribes.

PLATE P. 170

It would lead too far afield to discuss the other tribes or even groups of tribes in the same detail as the Iroquois. But it seems worth while to characterize them summarily before discussing their art. The Delaware, Mahican, Wappinger and other small confederations in the area of present-day New York State carried on intensive agriculture. Among the neighbouring groups to the north, who also belonged to the Algonquian family, hunting and fishing predominated. Maize was grown only in small fields and never provided more than a supplementary source of food. These groups include, among others, the Penobscot, Abnaki and Micmac. Another Algonquian group dwelling still farther north comprised the Naskapi, Cree and other tribes, who were nomadic hunters roaming their territory in small bands in search of caribou. Finally in the interior a separate group was formed by the Ojibwa (or Chippewa), Ottawa, Potawatomi, Miami, Sauk, Fox and Menomini (all Algonquian), together with the Sioux-speaking Winnebago. The economy of this group depended mainly upon the harvest of wild rice *(zizania aquatica)*, which grew around the Great Lakes and their tributaries. Maize was less essential here. Hunting and fishing remained important, however, and led to the adoption of many Plains traits, so that the Sauk, Fox and Miami belong rather to that area—in the discussion of which they have in fact already been mentioned.

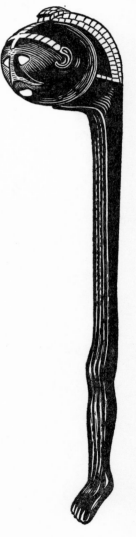

FIG. 71 – *Polished wooden club with shell inlay. The spherical end has been transformed into an expressively stylized head, the grip into a human leg. At the top is an animal covered with shells, possibly a snake. The club is a rare and outstanding early specimen of Indian wood carving. Iroquois, seventeenth century. Nationalmuseet, Copenhagen. Cf. p. 182.*

Birch-bark container with scratched-out naturalistic motifs. Animal motifs had a long history in the area of the upper Great Lakes, as can be seen from petroglyphs (cf. p. 23). Cree. *Length 28 cm. Denver Art Museum, Denver, Colo. Cf. p. 181.*

ART
Double-curve motif

Despite the diversity in language, economic forms and social structure, art shows a certain unity both in technique and motif, though of course some forms were more developed among certain groups than among others. Outstanding among the common motifs is the double curve. In its basic form this recalls a half-moon set on its back and provided with curling ends. Geographically, the central focus of the motif seems to lie among the Algonquian tribes on both sides of the lower St. Lawrence; it occurs in typical form, for example, among the Penobscot, who live in Maine. It was originally worked with elk hair on leather, but with the appearance of the Europeans these two materials were soon replaced by glass beads and cloth respectively, without altering the motifs in any essential way. On clothing (which was of European cut) cuffs, shoulder strips and parts of jackets were decorated in this technique. But the finest pieces are the collars and yokes with their carefully executed patterns. Similar work was done by the northerly neighbours of the Maine Penobscot, the Micmac of New Brunswick and the Passamaquoddy. The double-curve motif, which appears to be quite old, was not restricted to clothing. It was employed in wood carving as well, and appears on objects made of birch bark—boxes, canoes and the like. Stencils of folded birch bark were often used, into which the patterns would be bitten with the teeth. The caribou-hunting Naskapi in the interior of Labrador also knew the double curve, which they transformed by bending it up in the middle or breaking it up into segments. The motif is commonly found on coat-like garments of European cut made of caribou leather, on which it was painted in colours fixed with albumen from birds' eggs or fish. The neighbouring Montagnais also used the motif, though they frequently distorted it so that it became almost unrecognizable. The double curve was not restricted to the Algonquian tribes only, but spread far and wide, among the Iroquois, for example, where it sometimes disintegrated completely, and among the Huron. Offshoots reached as far as the Plains, where they can be studied among the Osage and other tribes.

PLATE P. 173

PLATE P. 175

Floral motifs

Flowers provided the source of another particularly important motif, ranking first among the Huron, Cree, Ojibwa, Menomini and other tribes of the Northeast. The double curve itself had a certain plant-like character and was often provided with stylized leaves, blossoms and buds. This close link between the two motifs suggests that they originally may have formed a unit that then developed along divergent paths. But this seems not to have been the case, for suggestions of the double curve had already appeared on mica and copper objects in the Hopewell period. None the less the appearance of plant ornament in the Northeast is noteworthy, in as much as such ornament played a distinctly minor role elsewhere in the art of North America

FIG. 72 – *War club of elk antler with the side not shown here inlaid with a rectangular mirror. Both sides bear naturalistic engravings, characteristic of the Northeast. This side shows two bison, two badgers with 'lines of communication' leading from the eyes, an under-water monster in the form of a snake with a fish tail and (the most important element) two so-called 'under-water panthers'. The latter rank among the most powerful spirits of the Northeast and the Great Plains. The deer is a later addition as is shown by the style. Winnebago, about 1839. After Eyman, 1963. Cf. pp. 181, 182.*

179

Birch-bark box decorated with coloured porcupine quills. These were not, as in other cases, done in appliqué technique on the surface but passed through the bark into the interior. The geometric patterns are also characteristic. Micmac. *Length 18.5 cm. Museum für Völkerkunde, Hamburg. Cf. pp. 181, 183.*

and in the New World as a whole; with few exceptions this category of decoration is due to European influence. Likewise, in the Northeast European flower patterns may have been copied and blended with the existing double curve motif. No final proof is at hand, though flower patterns have not yet been documented archaeologically; it is also known that Huron girls acquired European patterns in French convents in Canada, and introduced them into tribal art.

Two more motif groups must be mentioned here since they were important in the Northeast. One is geometric patterns which were much favoured among the Micmac, Iroquois and Cree. The other group, which comprises naturalistic renderings of living creatures, was common among the Cree, Montagnais and Iroquois, as well as among such Great Lakes tribes as the Menomini, Winnebago and Ojibwa. The animals—birds and a cat-like beast of mythological type described as an under-water panther—are mostly shown on flat surfaces, though they also appear three-dimensionally, especially among the Iroquois. In examining the Hopewell culture we have already seen that animal representations were a very old practice, a practice also noted (see chapter II) among the rock pictures of the Great Lakes, where they form an outstanding motif.

Even greater than the diversity of motifs was the diversity of technique used in the Northeast for the purpose of decoration. Some have already been mentioned, such as the use of birch bark, which served for stencils, tent coverings, vessels, baskets, boxes, canoes and so forth. In decorating these objects the templates were used as a guide in scratching out the unreserved surfaces so that a dark pattern appeared on a bright ground. Although a number of attempts have been made to link this area of diffusion with the Siberian one it seems rather that the easy employment of this material and the distribution of birch forests led to a parallel development. In connexion with birch bark we must mention the bark strips which the Ojibwa covered with incisions depicting men, animals and objects. In some cases these were 'magic-working' objects, to which recourse was had in various predicaments; others, especially the larger objects, depicted the songs of the Midewiwin society and were used as an aid to memory. In their class, these objects were the most advanced in the direction of a true

Other motif groups

PLATE P. 178

FIG. 70

FIG. 72

PLATE P. 22

Birch bark

PLATE P. 180

FIG. 73 – *Grip end of a Lacrosse ball bat in wood. The mixture of Indian and European elements, ideas and styles is particularly evident in this piece. Cayuga, before 1845. After Eyman, 1964. Cf. p. 182.*

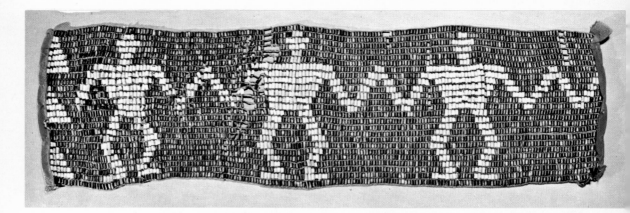

Wampum belt made of tubular shell beads ('wampum'). This belt represents a rare type, in as much as the ground is dark and the pattern light, the opposite of the normal procedure. Iroquois, eighteenth century. *Length 62 cm. Royal Ontario Museum, Toronto. Cf. p. 183.*

writing in pre-European North America. Their possible connexion with the rock pictures of the Great Lakes has already been mentioned.

Wood Wood was another favourite medium of the Northeast. Although in the absence of archaeological finds the development cannot be traced, the earliest known pieces show a remarkable mastery of form and material that suggests long familiarity with this art. Wood carving

FIG. 71 was widespread among the Iroquois: their clubs, crosses (ball-racquets),

FIG. 72 spoons, basins, etc., were decorated with animal motifs in both two and three dimensions. But here European motifs soon made their appearance; after 1800 the art of the Northeast was deeply contam-

FIG. 73 inated by this source. Among the Penobscot the double curve was dominant in wood as well as in the decoration of objects of horn and bone, while the bone combs of the Iroquois together with their small horn carvings bear stylized realistic figures.

In the preceding chapter it was pointed out that porcupine quill work probably originated in the Northeast. Generally the same objects were decorated as in the Plains—that is, primarily, objects of leather. But the types of decoration and pattern were quite different: double curves and flower motifs predominated, giving the patterns a more lively, floral appearance than is the case with the severe geometric ornaments of the Plains. A special place is occupied by the birch-bark boxes of the Micmac with their geometric patterns, for the quills were not applied in the usual manner, but drawn inside through holes and there turned down. Here we can appropriately speak of porcupine- PLATE P. 180 quill embroidery.

Closely related was another technique employing coloured elk hair. Here the decoration was not really embroidered, but applied as the quills customarily were and, in this case, secured with stitches; long chains were made by joining many short hairs bundled together. Although this kind of decoration was most highly developed among the Huron, it was also common to the other tribes living south of the St. Lawrence.

Although both techniques were largely displaced by the importation of European glass beads, they have lingered on to the present. The glass beadwork, which has already been alluded to, either retains old patterns or turns to plant motifs. The work of the Ojibwa is especially notewortly.

Beads were already known in pre-European times, but they were made *Wampum* of shell and often tubular. They were called wampum and are best known from the so-called 'wampum belts', in which white beads usually PLATE P. 182 formed the background with the pattern set off against them in violet. These belt-like strips had a symbolic character and were presented at the conclusion of treaties and on similar occasions. The best examples are the famous Penn belts, which are said to have marked the FIG. 74 confirmation of the treaty between William Penn and the Delaware in 1682. Of the figures shown on one belt the larger represents the Indian, the smaller the white man; this symbolized the friendship between the two groups and shows that the Indians considered themselves superior to the white man at that time. This relationship was soon to change, usually leading to the dissolution of Indian culture, of which only remnants have survived to our own day.

FIG. 74 – *'Wampum belt' of light and dark shell beads. It was given by the Delaware or Iroquois to William Penn, the founder of Pennsylvania, to mark the conclusion of a treaty. After Speck and Orchard, 1925. Cf. above.*

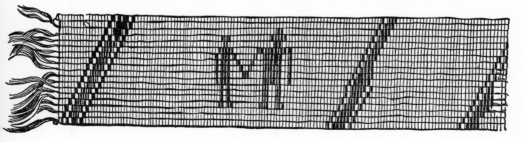

IX. THE SOUTHEAST

Geography   As indicated in the previous chapter, the northern boundary of the cultural region called the Southeast, customarily fixed at the northern limits of the present-day states of Tennessee and North Carolina, is actually uncertain and often theoretical. The situation in the west is also uncertain. We shall follow those scholars who annex areas west of the Mississippi, particularly in the coastal regions. By contrast, the eastern and southern boundaries are clearly set off by the Atlantic Ocean and the Gulf of Mexico.

The Southeast is environmentally not homogeneous. Climatic differences are, however, less important than topography and proximity to the sea. The southern part of the Appalachians enters like a wedge into the interior of this region, pushing forward the southern boundary of deciduous forests with their many oaks. Another important ecological formation is the pine forest zone along the Gulf coast. Apart from the Mississippi, a group of other rivers—the Tennessee, the Red River, the Tombigbee-Alabama system, the Chattahoochee and so forth—play an important part because of their broad alluvial valleys. Nor should one neglect the sharply indented, generally low coastline.

ARCHAEOLOGY   After the early stage of hunters attested by channelled projectile points found almost everywhere in North America, new traditions begin in the Southeast pointing forwards to a combined hunting and collecting economy—a system that lasts for a considerable time. It is, however, still uncertain whether the shell mounds on the coast and along the main rivers were only seasonal stations or whether they already represented specialized cultures with emphasis on molluscs as food.

The end of this 'Archaic' stage (as it is not very appropriately termed) is not the same in the various districts since it is marked by the appear-

Sandstone figure of a kneeling man, perhaps the finest example of its kind, which is distributed particularly in Tennessee. These objects are often felt to have a portrait-like quality. Spanish observers claim to have seen similar figures in temples, where they were possibly images of gods. Southern Cult. Found in a cave near Lebanon, Tenn. *Height 45 cm. Frank H. McCluny Museum, Knoxville, Tenn. Cf. p. 196.*

ance of ceramics. Fibre-tempered ceramics—a speciality of the South-east—appear as early as 1700 B.C. in some localities, e.g. the St. Johns River (Florida) and the Savannah River (Georgia). But no corresponding shift took place in the culture as a whole. In other districts the first pots appear only towards the beginning of our era. Possibly the early pottery, which occurs mainly in shell mounds, came from the north, though this is much disputed. In any case certain decorative forms that were to remain typical of these cultures—stamping, punctation and incisions—appear at this time.

During the first millennium B.C. influence from the north, particularly the Illinois-Ohio region, increased in the Appalachian area. But this never went beyond the bounds of the deciduous forest, in as much as acorns and nuts provided the main source of food. Stored in underground pits, acorns permitted bigger and more permanent settlements. Together with the acorn economy and possibly a new debittering process, it seems that the bow and arrow, a useful device for supplementing the food supply, came from the north with this 'Middle East' tradition, possibly accompanied by the custom of burying the dead in flexed position in round graves. The surface decoration of ceramics applied with a paddle that was carved or wrapped in coarse cloth undoubtedly represents an indigenous development. *'Middle East' tradition*

The influence from the north continued for a long time, though after about 500 B.C. it took on strong Adena and then Hopewell accents. Only rarely was this due to actual migration; more commonly it can be explained as the borrowing of ideas from areas with which contact had long been maintained. Typical is the appearance of burial mounds, platform pipes and copper ear spools in the Southeast and large conch shells imported from the Gulf Coast in the Northeast. These links are particularly evident in the first centuries of our era. About this time the first maize reached the Southeast; but, as at Hopewell, the growing of maize played a subordinate role, and the gathering of acorns seems to have easily retained its pre-eminence.

The Southern Appalachian tradition seems to have emerged directly from the Archaic stage about 500 B.C. The pottery shows clearly the *Southern Appalachian tradition*

Sandstone pipe. This outstanding piece, known as the 'lucifer pipe', reflects a naturalism characteristic of the figure sculpture of the period in which it was made. The old man, shown in typical kneeling position, is apparently sacrificing a deer. Southern Cult. Found at Spiro, Okla. *Height 19 cm. Stovall Museum, Norman, Okla. Cf. p. 197.*

FIG. 75 – *Curvilinear stamp pattern of a pottery vessel. Swift Creek phase, Southern Appalachian tradition. Found at Mandeville site, Georgia. After Kellar, Kelly and McMichael, 1962. Cf. below.*

special character of this tradition: the potters, no longer working their vessels up from a lump, adopted the spiral coiling technique. As temper, sand was employed instead of the ground soapstone favoured among the cultures influenced by Hopewell. The pottery is thinner than elsewhere. Characteristic is a pointed-base type, often with four small feet, accompanied by a fairly complicated stamped decoration. The latter was applied on the outside with a small wooden paddle when the pot was still wet, while a flat stone was pressed from within as a counter-force. Although the first paddles were wrapped with cord or cloth, later the patterns were cut directly on to the paddle's

FIG. 75   surface. Apart from parallel and crossing lines, complex curvilinear patterns are typical of this tradition through all periods.

We know little of other aspects of life in the Southern Appalachian tradition during the first centuries of its existence. It is certain that pottery spread far afield; in the first century of our era it covered the entire area between the upper Tennessee, the Atlantic, northern Florida and the Gulf Coast. Although the pottery is homogeneous, other aspects present a mixed picture, with an acorn economy in the forest zone and a shell economy on the coast, both augmented by what appears to be a rudimentary type of horticulture. While burial mounds appear in the north, other areas retained the old round graves. Everything points to the conclusion that we are dealing with the diffusion of ideas, not with conquests or migrations.

Gulf tradition   Before the beginning of our era another tradition which seems to have originated on the lower Mississippi made itself felt. Typical of the Tchefuncte culture (regarded as the source) are pots that are punctated, zoned, incised and rocker stamped. During the following phases these beginnings were enlarged through a growing Hopewell influence as well as internal developments to produce elaborate burial customs. At the same time the Gulf tradition, as it is now called, expanded forcefully. By about A.D. 500 it had occupied the whole coastal belt as far as northern Florida and Georgia, together with a large stretch west of the Mississippi, the so-called Caddo area, which includes southern Arkansas, northern Louisiana, eastern Texas and Oklahoma. The Gulf tradition seems to have had an agricultural base, but there are still survivals of older economic forms varying according to region and state of development. Except when used in religious ceremonies, pottery tended to retain the forms of older practice. Therefore the pots of southern Georgia and northern Florida continued to be stamped. In this case, too, we must assume that the Gulf tradition mirrors the spread of a religious and social pattern over the whole coastal region between eastern Texas and the Atlantic coast of Georgia, without significantly affecting the old ways.

Proof of this is furnished by the most typical features of the tradition: burial mounds, sometimes with multiple graves, and temple platforms. Differences in grave furniture suggest that a system of social rank went hand in hand with these customs. Analogies to these facts could still be observed among the historical Natchez of Louisiana and Timucua of Florida, for example: social classes, emphasis on ancestry, privileges for the nobility, sacrifice of retainers of deceased nobles and so forth. These later cultures were probably rooted in the old Gulf

Stone pipe in the form of a parrot or an owl. The shape is typical of the tobacco pipes in animal form that were in use during or shortly after the end of the Southern Cult. Found in Tennessee. *Length 29 cm. Brooklyn Museum, Brooklyn, N. Y. Cf. p. 197.*

tradition. That a certain religious uniformity existed is proved by small copper masks of a long-nosed god found both in Florida and Oklahoma. One of the disputed questions about the Gulf tradition is whether the idea of the temple platform was indigenous or was introduced from elsewhere. Since burial mounds were previously known in the tradition, it is quite conceivable that they gave rise to the temple platform. Somewhat similarly, the spread of maize, possibly accompanied by beans and pumpkins, may have proceeded along indigenous lines after an early importation from the north. It is more difficult, however, to explain other things in terms of indigenous development, such as the bottle-like shape of pots and the fine-lined incision decor applied after firing, both of which occur in the Caddo area, as well as the negative painting techniques and the pots in the shape of animals and fruits found in Florida. These things point to a link with Meso-America, reinforcing the possibility that the ideas of the temple platform and of social rank also came from Mexico. The route taken by this influence is contested. One possible channel, which could account for parallels in the Caddo area, runs through the Gilmore corridor in north-eastern Mexico and Texas. Groups in this region who migrated seasonally could have carried ideas and individual objects from one end of the corridor to another. But this route does not explain the isolated appearance of specific Meso-American traits in Florida. Here we may have to reckon with maritime links.

Middle Mississippi tradition Towards A.D. 1000 the Southeast shows certain common features which were part of the Gulf tradition, but at the same time individual variations occurred and many small units had developed. The long-standing and important influence from the north disappeared and the ideas it had brought were transformed. However, this situation changed under pressure of the advancing Mid dle Mississippi tradition mentioned in the previous chapter. This tradition probably developed from Meso-American ideas that travelled across the Caddo area mixed with lingering elements of the old Hopewell tradition. A new feature is the fact that not only did the Indians of the Middle Mississippi tradition export their ideas, as happened elsewhere, but they took possession of large areas by migration and conquest. Possibly we are witnessing the spread of the Muskogee and Sioux language families. This powerful and successful expansion rested on an economic foundation of new strains of maize and new methods of cultivation—both apparently derived from Meso-America. Consequently, the settlements were located in or near broad alluvial river-bottoms, favourable for agriculture. Every district had at least one big settlement often

FIG. 76 – *Buff pottery vessel in the form of a human head, possibly the portrait of a dead man. The holes in the ears served for the attachment of rings in some other material. Southern Cult complex. Found at Fortune Mound, Arkansas. After Douglas and D'Harnoncourt, 1941. Cf. pp. 192, 195.*

called a 'town'. This was always fortified and arranged around a large plaza with one or more temple platforms erected of earth on a square or rectangular base. The unstepped sides sometimes had a smooth clay facing. A ramp or flight of steps of earth or clay led up to the temples and/or chiefs' dwellings, constructed of perishable materials, on the flat top. Both the temples and the numerous houses within the fortifications were rectangular with a frame consisting of thin vertically placed poles with their ends bent in and woven together so as to form a flattened dome. Reed mats were attached to both sides of the walls and plastered externally with clay. The roof was covered with grass. Apart from these 'towns', smaller open settlements existed; these appear to have been politically and spiritually dependent on the 'towns'.

The Middle Mississippi tradition did not spread out uniformly as a compact unit, but restricted itself to favourable areas (primarily to broad river valleys), where it often coexisted with remnants of older cultures. In this way we can account for the wide diffusion of the tradition, which is found near St. Louis and in central Wisconsin, as well as in central and southern Georgia, Tennessee and Florida. Moreover, this factor explains why the groups participating in the tradition diverged so greatly; by about A.D. 1400 the underlying unity can scarcely be recognized. Nevertheless a common link must have subsisted in some sense so as to permit the spread of one idea—to be discussed below. In the field of art this tradition and this period as a whole are somewhat unrewarding, for even the pottery becomes monotonous. Characteristic features are spherical shapes and lugs for suspension cords, as well as tempering with ground shells. Decoration is generally absent with the exception of simple cord impressions, but sometimes older decorative forms persisted on a local basis. The only artistic innovations of this period are small modelled heads on the rims of bowls and the spread of positive and negative painted decorations which were already known.

We have mentioned that a new idea spread over the Southeast around *Southern cult* A.D. 1400. This was not restricted to the area of the southern settlements of the Mississippi tradition, but spread much farther. In fact with one exception, Moundville in Alabama, its most important known centres lie outside the tradition. They include Etowah in Georgia, where the everyday pottery suggests an affiliation with the Southern Appalachian tradition; Mount Royal in Florida, a part of the Gulf tradition; and Spiro in Oklahoma, in the old Caddo area. All these main centres are extensive settlements, which can be properly called towns. In each case their cultural basis, including the temple platforms, follow their ancestral tradition, on to which the new ideas appear to have been grafted. This complex is termed the Southern Cult or Southern Death Cult. It embraces ritual objects, symbols, images and art styles, all clearly having a religious meaning. Its origin has not yet been fully clarified, but in all likelihood the beginnings lie in the Caddo area of Texas and Oklahoma, where remnants of the old Gulf tradition fused with fresh Meso-American contributions to form the Southern Cult. It is certain that Meso-America was the source of many traits associated with the cult; the starting point can be fixed more exactly in the coastal regions of the Huaxtecs in northern Veracruz and Tamaulipas. For this reason sea-borne contact has often been suggested, but it is now certain that the situation can be largely accounted for by the passage of ideas only—not the objects themselves—across the Gilmore corridor to the Southeast. This explains why many objects (e.g. shell disks) recall Mexican prototypes without being identical with them and why style elements converge that are not associated in their Mexican homeland. These facts demonstrate that only concepts and styles were borrowed, to be transformed in accordance with indigenous ways of thinking.

Motifs

The inventory of objects comprising the Southern Cult is very large and the materials used are quite varied. But a certain unity of style and a canon of motifs do exist. Conditioned by the materials, the motifs are depicted in different ways, but they constantly recur.

FIGS. 76, 83
FIG. 81

A broad area is occupied by images of the dead, mostly in the form of skulls appearing either alone or held by men. They suggest that skull trophies were important in religious rites. Other symbols of the dead are bones of the upper arm, which are also prominent in Mexican art, fleshless forearms and hands. Another important group of motifs is that of eyes. Among these the 'forked-eye motif' consists of an eye

FIG. 77 – *Stone disk with engraved knotted rattlesnakes surrounding a hand-and-eye motif. Southern Cult complex. Found at Moundville, Alabama. After Fundaburk and Foreman, 1957. Cf. pp. 194, 196.*

Diorite bowl in the form of a duck. Because of its preservation and execution, elegant lines and blend of abstraction and realism, this piece ranks among the finest art works of the Southeastern United States. Southern Cult. Found at Moundville, Hale County, Ala. *Length 25.4 cm. Museum of the American Indian, Heye Foundation, New York, N. Y. Cf. p. 197.*

FIG. 78 – *Circular pendant of shell. The engraved decoration consists of a sun symbol enclosed by a banded square with four woodpecker heads. Southern Cult complex. Found in Limestone County, Alabama. After Fundaburk and Foreman, 1957. Cf. below and p. 199.*

FIG. 77

FIG. 78

FIGS. 77, 80

FIG. 81

FIG. 79

Materials

drawn in rather naturalistic fashion with a frame showing two or three points. These are often interpreted either as traces of tears or as an indication of the flashing eye of the thunder bird, but more probably represent the eye-markings of certain falcons. Another favourite motif couples a naturalistic eye with a hand, the eye usually being placed on the palm of the hand. In its strong stylization the motif of the 'open eye' contrasts with the others mentioned; it recalls a real eye only vaguely. Another motif can be regarded as an eye, specifically as the closed eye of the dead. Because of its form, an oval enclosing a central bar, it is called a 'barred oval'. According to the context it may be interpreted as an anus or a vagina. Another widely diffused motif is the cross, which appears in various forms: simple cross, swastika, whorl. Though the cross can also stand alone, it tends to be enclosed in a circle. In this form it recalls yet another important motif, the 'sun circle', with which it is often interchangeable. 'Sun circles' take varied forms: they may have smooth, notched or scalloped edges and crosses, whorls, circles or eyes in the centre. Finally we must mention the bi-lobed arrow, whose main element is an arrow pointing downwards flanked by two kidney-shaped objects.

All these motifs may appear either singly or in combination, or else integrated into larger compositions. They may be component parts or attributes of men and animals, though these appear to have divine status. As well as human beings, feline animals, birds (eagles and woodpeckers) and rattlesnakes are depicted. A common practice is to blend the different species so as to produce eagle-headed men, winged and/or horned snakes and so forth. The symbolic character of all these beings makes it likely that magico-religious considerations determined their make-up.

The many ritual objects with which we are concerned are best classified according to the materials used. Clay of course was one of them,

FIG. 79 – *Winged snake. Engraving on a pottery vessel from Moundville, Alabama. Southern Cult complex. After Fundaburk and Foreman, 1957. Cf. above and p. 195.*

FIG. 80 – *Circular shell pendant with engraving of a rattlesnake. Southern Cult complex. Found at McMahan Mound, Sevierville, Tennessee. After Holmes, 1883. Cf. pp. 194, 199.*

but it did not occupy a very prominent place and was commonly overshadowed by other materials. However, the bottle-shaped pots must be mentioned. In their simplest form they derive from the Middle Mississippi tradition and from the Caddo area, but they were diffused by the cult complex into regions untouched by these two traditions. They can be distinguished from older forms by the motifs mentioned above. Both positive and negative painting techniques were important. Other pottery forms include double and triple vases, sometimes with stirrup spouts. Especially noteworthy are vessels taking the form of heads of the dead; striking in their naturalism, they rank among the finest ceramics of the Southeast. Regional variations can be distinguished in the pottery. Thus the pieces from Moundville are generally decorated with incisions, among which ritual motifs, especially winged snakes, are important. Moundville also created such special designs as wave bands.

FIG. 82
FIG. 76

FIG. 79

In the Southern Cult area stone objects were much more important than pottery. Among these are the finely chipped flint blades reaching up to three feet in length. These, as well as clubs, 'eagle claws', disks and 'tortoises' made from the same material and in the same technique were found especially on the Duck River in Tennessee. The last-named forms, the purpose of which is still unknown, strongly recall the 'eccentric flints' of the Maya area, but no real link can be proved. Other ceremonial objects were the monolithic stone axes whose blade and grip form a single piece. Like the so-called command batons, which are mainly known from pictorial scenes, they were probably symbols of rank. Similarly, the big celts generally made of soft stone and without a cutting edge seem to have had no practical purpose. The 'spuds' appearing in connexion with the Southern Cult—stone instruments with a long thin shaft and a broad, often semi-circular blade—as well as pierced axe blades can already be found in preceding phases and periods; they clearly mark the persistence of older traditions.

Stone

FIG. 81 – *Copper plate in the form of an eagle-man. The left hand holds a human head with a 'forked eye', the right a rattle. A 'bi-lobed arrow symbol' surmounts the head-dress. Southern Cult complex. Found in Etowah, Georgia. After Willoughby, 1932. Cf. pp. 192, 194, 200.*

Wooden alligator head. The original white, black and blue painting has greatly faded since its discovery in 1895. The head and lower jaw are separate and must originally have been hinged. Calusa (?). Found at Key Marco, Fla. *Length 25 cm. University Museum, Philadelphia, Pa. Cf. p. 201.*

Although the use of all these objects is still not very clear, we are well informed about the purpose of the stone disks that are often hollowed out in a bowl-like fashion and occasionally pierced. They were used to play *chungke*, a game still popular in historical times among the Cree and other tribes. These stones must not be confused with the FIG. 77 stone disks generally known as palettes, whose purpose is uncertain, though their often rich incised decoration suggests that they must have been ceremonial objects. They are usually round, rarely rectangular and with their generally jagged or scalloped edges recall the sun circle motif, which they may represent. We have now reached PLATE P. 184 the finest stone products of the Southern Cult. Foremost among these are the relatively rare, often outstanding human figures. Crouching or kneeling, they reveal on the whole a pronounced naturalism that has a portrait-like quality. Who was represented and what the purpose of these figures was is still uncertain. They have been found especially in Tennessee, but are known also from Kentucky, Georgia, Mississippi and Illinois. Even rarer are individual stone heads or masks that often FIG. 83 give the impression of a death mask. The stone figures themselves are closely related to large stone pipes, where kneeling men are also a favourite motif. As with the other stone objects the most varied kinds of stone were used, though for pipes red sandstone (catlinite) is common. These pipes are noteworthy not only for their artistic quality, but also because of the fact that those depicting human figures show them during activities which give us some insight into ceremonial life. Smokers and *chungke* players were shown; a famous piece from Spiro PLATE P. 186 seems to point to human sacrifice; another shows the sacrifice of a stag. Pipes in the shape of animals are also rather common. Birds and PLATE P. 189 frogs appear frequently, while pumas, snakes and shrimps are less common. In as much as they are often isolated finds, the dating of these pipes remains uncertain. They may belong to the Southern Cult or they may be somewhat later, forming a transition to the smaller pipes of historical times. Animal forms were also used to decorate stone bowls, which also belonged to the Cult. Among them sculpture and relief are fused together, though not in the piece that ranks as one of the most famous examples of North American Indian art from pre-European times—a diorite bowl in the form of a duck from Moundville. PLATE P. 193 Colour, execution and proportions combine to give it an unusual beauty that is hard to match among comparable pieces. Finally pendants and similar objects were made of stone and often decorated with ritual motifs.

Because of the methods of handling, shell-work can be linked with *Shell* stone. Shell was favoured in the Southern Cult, where objects made of it are sometimes of outstanding quality. This was not the case with the products of earlier workers of the material. A group of particular interest is that of the so-called 'pectoral masks', produced from portions of a big conch shell, often tapering towards the bottom, or revealing the original form in some other way. The faces depicted consist of a mouth and nose in flat relief, pierced eyes and an incised hair-line

FIG. 82 – *Pottery figure of a kneeling man painted in red and buff. Southern Cult complex. Found at Arkansas Post, Arkansas. After Dockstader, 1962. Cf. p. 195.*

Feline, possibly a puma, in wood. This Egyptian-looking figure ranks among the most beautiful objects known from pre-European America. Calusa (?). Found at Key Marco, Fla. *Height 15 cm. U. S. National Museum, Washington, D. C. Cf. p. 201.*

FIG. 83 – *Mask-like face in white stone, possibly representing a dead man. Southern Cult complex. Found in Gallatin County, Kentucky. After Douglas and D'Harnoncourt, 1941. Cf. pp. 192, 197.*

and eye-markings—the last commonly in the form of the 'forked-eye motif'. These mask-like objects which produce an abstract effect have been found on the face or chest of the dead. Since there are no holes for attachment, except for the eyes, nor any considerable traces of use, it has been thought that they are grave goods pure and simple. Whole figures of shell are uncommon, but they tend to be of high quality. The bulk of the shell objects of the Southern Cult consists of disks with two holes at the top for suspension on a necklace. As material the Indians used big conch shells, exposing the rosy hues of the inside to view. Besides smooth edged pieces there appear less frequently fretted or notched examples that again relate the disks to the 'sun motif'. The decorations inside were incised or cut out, the two methods often being combined. Because of the large number of these disks that have been found a plethora of motifs can be singled out. But the complexity can be reduced by linking them on one hand to the motifs previously mentioned and on the other by classifying them in groups. A good many have a cross, concentric circles or a spiral as the main motif, though the design may often be so elaborated as to be scarcely recognizable. A widespread type shows a 'sun motif' in the centre, FIG. 78 enclosed by a square formed by an endless ribbon with a loop at each corner and a stylized woodpecker head on each side. Patterns based FIG. 80 on spirals were easily transformed into coiled rattlesnakes. Spiders were linked to concentric circles and facing woodpeckers were joined by a cross. Important in connexion with religion are the stylized representations of composite creatures with human and bird features. But the most interesting, and artistically most valuable, incision patterns are those of human beings, who are depicted in varied, often quite active attitudes. Thus they may be *chungke* players; dancers with an eagle mask (often holding a human head in their hands); groups of dancers, generally quite stiff and holding rattles; and, also in pairs, warriors in combat. This art fascinates not only because of the careful

FIG. 84 – *Shell 'mask'. The zigzag lines on the cheeks, often described as 'tear tracks', are more probably a modification of the 'forked-eye motif'. Southern Cult complex. Found in Stafford County, Virginia. After Fundaburk and Foreman, 1957. Cf. pp. 192, 199.*

FIG. 85 – *Cedar mask representing a 'deer-man' or a man wearing deer antlers, a popular motif. The eyes, mouth and (originally) the ear plugs are inlaid with shell. Southern Cult complex. Found at Spiro, Oklahoma. After Burnett, 1945. Cf. p. 201.*

execution, the lively movement, the rich details indicating ornaments, clothing and religious objects, but also because of the wealth of ideas and the sure sense of form revealed in the careful composition of the scenes within the space provided by the circular pieces. Even finer and more vital are the incised patterns on the outer surfaces of big conch shells that were cut in half so as to form dippers, though perhaps they were intended specifically to hold ritual potions similar to the 'black drink' of the Muskogee tribes. These conch shells were richly decorated at Etowah and especially at Spiro, where hundreds of fragments were found. Since a large surface was available the groups could be well developed, more details added and the action made more lively. Apart from creatures resembling human beings and ritual motifs, the patterns frequently include winged snakes and stylized trees—a unique plant motif in the Southeast.

Copper

FIG. 81

Human figures, sometimes with eagle masks or heads, together with eagles themselves, comprise the chief motifs of thin copper plates on to which patterns were embossed in low relief. The outer contours were generally cut out. These copper plates seem to have been used in certain rites, for all means of attachment are lacking. By contrast, square copper plates showing human faces and/or the 'forked-eye motif' may have served as the forehead piece of a head-dress. Circular pectorals, similar to those made of shell, were also produced from copper, their motifs being restricted to the cross, swastika and whorl.

FIG. 81

Another group of ornaments made from thin copper sheets consists of 'hairpins' in the shape of feathers, command batons, and 'bi-lobed arrows'. The way these were worn is easy to determine from figures shown in scenes. Other thin copper objects seem to have been worn on clothing or used as neck ornaments. Like the hairpins, these may have been symbols of rank. Sheet copper was also used to encase or decorate such wood or stone objects as flint blades, circular pendants and coiled ear-rings. The latter were also made wholly out of copper. They represent a last echo from the period of Northern Woodland

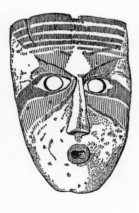

FIG. 86 – *Mask in painted wood. Found at Key Marco, Florida. After Cushing, 1897. Cf. p. 201.*

influence, when they entered the Southeast together with the technique of working copper in the cold state—though this only now reached full development. The only massive copper objects of the Southern Cult were big celts, apparently of ritual significance.

This religious aspect is highlighted by some pieces that were found *Wood* at Spiro together with their wooden shafts. Here the back of the blade protrudes from the open beak of a bird, whose eyes are inlaid on the shaft in shell. Wood must have been a very important medium in the Southern Cult, but since it is rarely preserved we can only speculate as to how it was worked. The majority of the pieces preserved come from Spiro. Apart from the above-mentioned axe handles they include human masks with eyes, eyelashes and mouths inlaid in shell and occasionally with antlers carved from the same piece of wood, as well as small masks of naturalistic form, animal figures and trays with *FIG. 85* incised ornaments.

In this connexion another important find must be mentioned that, *Key Marco* though it does not properly belong to the period of the Southern Cult, was influenced by it to a certain degree. In 1884 a cache of over a hundred wooden objects was discovered in the mud of Key Marco off the coast of Florida. It is the largest group of objects of this kind found in North America, the Arctic excepted. The objects have been ascribed to the historical Calusa Indians, who lived in south-western Florida and whose economy was primarily oriented to the sea. These numerous, often artistically carved ornaments are inlaid with tiny bits of tortoise shell and sea shell. Painting also appears occasionally. For us, the so-called 'ceremonial objects' are of special interest. Among these are some rather animated masks in the form of human faces— always with careful painting—as well as tablets carved and painted with abstract designs, and boards and chest-lids painted with naturalistic figures in lively attitudes. The finest pieces artistically are some small animal heads whose purpose is unknown; because of their combination and realism they must be ranked among the best art works produced by North American Indians. Together with heads of birds, tortoises and alligators, there appear heads of mammals—wolves, deer and perhaps opossum. In every case the effect of carving is enhanced by painting, generally in black and yellow (or white). It is somewhat arbitrary to single out one object from the mass as the finest, but the figure of a feline animal, possibly a puma, seems to cry out

FIG. 87 – *Small human figure in shell. Southern Cult complex. Found at Spiro, Oklahoma. After Fundaburk and Foreman, 1957. Cf. p. 199.*

for mention. Although it is only about 6 inches high, it conveys an impression of concentrated power which certainly made it a ritual object of first rank among the Indians. The figure's attitude, which recalls that of Egyptian statuary, the balance of the whole composition and the unsurpassable realism give it unique value as a work of art, worthy to be mentioned with the great art treasures of the Old and New World.

With Key Marco we have left the age of the Southern Cult, which faded away in the seventeenth century, to enter the historical period, which will only be discussed briefly here. Many of the numerous tribes of the Southeast may be traced back to archaeological phases and cultures; an example is the Natchez, who appear to have retained many elements of the Gulf tradition. Moreover, a link seems to exist between the Middle Mississippi tradition, the Southern Cult and the tribes of the Muskogee language family (Choctaw, Chickasaw, Creek, Seminoles, possibly Calusa, and others). Customs deriving from the Southern Cult may also have persisted among the Iroquoian Cherokee where (as among the Muskogee tribes) they are reflected, for example, in the New Year festival known as the Great Busk, which is celebrated at the summer solstice.

Cherokee The Cherokee, who occupied much of North and South Carolina, Tennessee and Georgia, represent not only the largest Indian group of the Southeast, with an estimated population of 20,000 around A.D. 1600, but rank among the region's most advanced peoples. They lived in villages and towns with up to 200 huts distributed around a central plaza with its temple and council houses, an arrangement we have already noted in the Middle Mississippi tradition. The houses with their rectangular plan reflect this tradition as well, while the council houses had seven sides, with a central post surrounded by three concentric circles of seven posts each. Seven was a sacred number among the Cherokee and it recurs constantly. The social organization comprised seven matrilinear clans; seven heavens and seven directions were recognized; and there were seven important festivals of which six recurred annually and the last was held every seven years. The number seven was important in political life too, for the chief was assisted by seven high officials: the spokesman, the 'right-hand man' and five councillors. While the chief combined political and religious authority, military affairs were in the hands of the Chief Warrior,

Gourd mask. This object, consisting of two pieces, is decked out with fur and partially painted in black. It was used in the 'booger dance'. Cherokee, twentieth century. *Height 24.4 cm. The University Museum, Philadelphia, Pa. Cf. p. 204.*

FIG. 89 — *Basket in split black, red and yellow reed. The pattern is known as 'worm tracks'. Chitimacha. After Merwin, 1919. Cf. below.*

aided by three officials and seven councillors. In the council of warriors an important role was played by the *agiyagasta* or 'honoured lady', who gave her opinion on important questions of peace and war; this shows the high status of women among the Cherokee. Villages and towns had their own military, political and religious organizations, which were, however, subject to the appropriate tribal bodies. The main source of food came from intensive cultivation of maize, beans, pumpkins, squashes, sunflowers and tobacco. Hunting was important for meat and was commonly carried out with blow-guns. Originally clothing was made either of leather or of woven or knotted fibre from mulberries and other plants sewn on to a bark-cloth foundation. These garments, which are said to have been of great beauty, were inevitably driven out by trade in European textiles, which the Indians decorated in various ways. Other craft products included fine basketry work made from split reeds in sundry colours (common among many tribes of the Southeast), figurally decorated tobacco-pipes made from black stone, and especially wood carving, including potters' paddles, pipe tubes, drums and three-dimensional masks painted or decorated with skins. While the wooden masks were quite naturalistic, those made of gourds were stylized. The pottery vessels, which displayed geometric patterns, were beaten with wooden paddles.

FIG. 89

FIG. 88

PLATE P. 203

We cannot leave the Southeast and the Cherokee without mentioning a post-European event that throws light on the high achievements of the Cherokee: the invention of a syllabic script by the half-breed Indian Sequoyah in 1821. This did not develop into the privileged possession of a small elite, but became an object of such popular enthusiasm that illiteracy was stamped out among the Cherokee in a few years. The Cherokee issued a newspaper in this script, written and printed by them. But neither this success, nor the formation of a government on the American model with two houses of delegates, nor yet the request to be admitted as a state to the American union was any use to the Cherokee in the end. Together with the other 'civilized tribes' of the Southeast—the Choctaw, Chickasaw, Creek and Seminoles—they were driven out of their flourishing villages in the 1830's and resettled in Oklahoma. Thus the flourishing culture of the Indians of the Southeast was extinguished, closing one of the darkest chapters in the encounter of Indians and Whites.

APPENDIX: THE WEST INDIES

The chain of islands that stretches from North to South America, *Geography* separating the Gulf of Mexico and the Caribbean Sea from the Atlantic Ocean, is generally divided into three parts: the Bahamas, the Greater Antilles (Cuba, Hispaniola, Puerto Rico and Jamaica) and the Lesser Antilles. We will be primarily concerned with the Greater Antilles, where a particular artistic development took place; the other two parts will be mentioned only in passing.

The West Indies do not belong to North America either archaeolog- *Ciboney* ically or ethno-linguistically; rather they constitute an offshoot of the South American cultural area extending far to the north. At one time scholars believed that the earliest stratum of indigenous people, the Ciboney, who at the time of the Spanish conquest were living in western Cuba and the Guaicayarima peninsula of Haiti, had originally migrated from Florida, but this assumption proved to be unfounded. Today it is held that the earliest pre-ceramic cultures, which appeared in the south before the time of Christ and in the north in the Christian era and which (as in other periods) have different names in the various islands (e.g. Couri and Cabaret in Haiti, Cayo Redondo and Guayabo Blanco in western Cuba), came from Venezuela and perhaps also from Central America. Possessing a minimal material culture, these people lived mostly in caves and rock shelters, and occasionally under the protection of wind screens. Their food was obtained from the coasts and sea.

The next group of people, who moved from Venezuela to the West *Pre-Arawak* Indies and who are called Sub-Taino or Pre-Arawak, had already known agriculture in their homeland, where they cultivated a South American tuberous plant called manioc. Their permanent settlements stood near the sea or along the lower courses of rivers, seemingly located for convenient access to the sea, which provided a food supplement. These groups, which stem from the Barrancas-Saladero tradition of Venezuela, are traceable about the beginning of our era in Trinidad and Grenada, whence they gradually spread north-west following the chain of islands. Together with agriculture, they brought ceramics, either painted white on red or with grooved engravings. The groups known as the Arawak also seem to have migrated to the *Arawak*

206

Wooden stool *(duho)*. The broad end curves up to form a back-like part. From the lower end a carved human head projects. The incised curvilinear decoration is in the typical Taino style. Found in a cave near La Patana, Cuba. *Length 38.7 cm. Museum of the American Indian, Heye Foundation, New York, N. Y. Cf. p. 209.*

Andesite head in the form of a skull. It probably represents the head of a man-like *zemi* with its characteristic round eye sockets. Taino culture. Found in the Greater Antilles. *Height 22 cm. Musée de l'Homme, Paris. Cf. p. 209.*

207

FIG. 90 – *Modelled human head from a pottery vessel. Taino culture. Found in the Dominican Republic. Museum für Völkerkunde, Hamburg. Cf. below.*

West Indies from the same area. Their beginnings in the south-eastern part of the island chain can be placed at about A.D. 700. They were agriculturalists as well. They did not live exclusively on the coast but also settled in the interior of the islands. They were evidently less dependent on the sea.

Taino These Arawak formed the basis for a development first evident in the Ostiones phase on Puerto Rico; later this spread to eastern Cuba, Hispaniola and the Virgin Islands. As in the Southern Cult of the Southeast we are certainly confronted here with a ceremonial complex with components indicating Meso-American influences. Maize, which took second place to manioc in the economy, a strong chieftainship and social stratification are aspects of this complex, which is called the Taino culture after a tribe encountered by Columbus. Large ball-courts are characteristic features in the villages of this culture. Moreover, many art objects are linked to the ceremonial complex, again paralleling what we have seen in the Southeast. Pottery is the least interesting of the artistic products. The Indians of the Taino culture preferred dishes and bottles, which were generally provided with a grooved geometric decoration. Moreover, appliqué faces in typically stylized form were fixed to the rims of dishes and on necks of bottles. More

FIG. 90 important were objects made from sea shells, a material that had been used from the time of the first settlements for tools and utensils—choppers, hatchet blades, vessels etc. But at this stage it underwent an artistic elaboration. Apart from small pendants of various types craftsmen made masks and rings adorned with figures. Bone was used to make small figures and spatulas with decorated ends.

Stone Still more developed was the art of stone working. Among the many objects made from this material the *zemi* must be mentioned first. They were regarded as the seat of personal spirits, and were thought

FIG. 91 – *Pendant in greenish stone in the form of a crocodile zemi head. Taino culture. Found in the Dominican Republic. Museum für Völkerkunde, Hamburg. Cf. p. 209.*

to be imbued with great power. Although *zemi* could be made in any material, stone seems to have been particularly favoured. The *zemi* commonly take the form of a human figure or head, but may also show animal forms: birds, frogs and crocodiles. Typical of the human type are the bent legs and the projecting head, which gives the figure a distinctly hunchback-like appearance. Like the other representations of men, which cannot be securely identified as *zemi*, the faces have big round eyes, which must originally have been inlaid. This is also probably true of the large round ear-plugs, another characteristic feature. In some cases the noses are depicted without flesh so that one is reminded of a skull. In other specimens one finds the features of an old man—in whole figures joined to an emaciated body with projecting ribs and vertebrae. There is great variation in the size of *zemi* figures, ranging from important pieces kept by the chiefs in special huts to charms worn by men on the forehead in time of war. Also connected with the ceremonial complex are 'three-pointed stones', sometimes displaying a human face, and stone rings with geometric patterns. But the exact function of both remains uncertain.

FIG. 91

Stone was also used to make monolithic axes recalling those of the Southeast, tear-shaped celts with human figures in low relief and pestles, the upper parts of which were worked in the form of a human or animal head or figure. Finally in this connexion we must mention the pictographs that go back to earlier times, though they show typical features of the Taino style.

FIGS. 94, 95

Another apparent high point of Taino art was wood carving, though only a few objects in this medium have been preserved. Among them are deep seats or oval stools, sometimes provided with a projection at the back. They are decorated with carved heads and incised patterns of a curved geometric type. In some cases the stool is trans-

FIG. 94 – *Green stone pestle in the shape of a hunchbacked man. Taino culture. Found in the Dominican Republic. Museum für Völkerkunde, Hamburg. Cf. p. 209.*

formed into a representation of an animal or a man. Wooden *zemi* figures are also known and among these eyes, ear-plugs and teeth are commonly inlaid with shell.

Caribs   In conclusion we must briefly mention that from about A.D. 1200 a new wave of immigrants moved into the Antilles from South America. By 1500 they had already occupied all the Lesser Antilles, when European discovery and conquest put an end to their expansion. The Caribs seem to have been plunderers and fishermen rather than farmers. Consequently their products are scanty and need not be treated here.

FIG. 95 – *Pestle in light brown and black-veined stone, decorated at the upper end with a human head. Taino culture. Found in the Dominican Republic. Museum für Völkerkunde, Hamburg. Cf. p. 209.*

APPENDIX

BIBLIOGRAPHY

Note: Scholarly literature on the North American Indians and their past is enormous. Even if we confine our attention to books and articles devoted to describing and illustrating art objects in the usual sense of the term the list would still be too long, for the small archaeological and ethnological journals—of which there are over one hundred in the United States alone—publish many important contributions, for example, *The Masterkey* of the Southwest Museum in Los Angeles, the *Florida Anthropologist* of Gainesville and *El Palacio* of Santa Fé, N. M., to mention only a few. So it is hard to decide what to include. Any choice is subjective to the extent that it is conditioned by the habits and preferences of the author as well as by the accidents that bring this or that item into his hands. The author takes full responsibility for any omissions and asks for patient understanding of anything that may have been overlooked. The following list includes fundamental books treating North America in general or a particular region. Many of these books, especially the recent ones, provide extensive bibliographies. In addition books are included that deal with the art of a substantial area or clarify a special technique. A third category comprises items relating to one or more of the objects illustrated in this volume.

The entries are arranged in accordance with the chapters of the book, but it was sometimes unavoidable that a book which covers ground treated in two or more chapters be mentioned only once. This is especially true of the Northeast and Southeast; works that concern these two regions appear under the Northeast.

I. GENERAL

Adam, Leonhard: Primitive Art; rev. and enlarged ed., Penguin Books A 67, Harmondsworth, 1949.

Ashton, Dore: Abstract Art before Columbus; André Emmerich Gallery, New York, 1957.

Boas, Franz: Primitive Art; Instituttet for Sammenlignende Kulturforskning, ser. b, no. 12, Oslo, 1927; repr. Dover Publications, New York, 1956.

Christensen, Erwin O.: Primitive Art; Viking Press, New York, 1955.

Covarrubias, Miguel: The Eagle, the Jaguar, and the Serpent; Alfred A. Knopf, New York, 1954.

D'Harcourt, Raoul: Arts de l'Amérique; Arts du Monde, Paris, 1948; Eng. transl., A. Rosin, Primitive Art of the Americas, 1950.

D'Harnoncourt, René: El arte del indio en los Estados Unidos; The National Indian Institute, U. S. Department of the Interior, Washington, 1943.

Dockstader, Frederick J.: Indian Art in America; New York Graphic Society, Greenwich, Conn., 2nd rev. ed., 1962.

Douglas, Frederic H. and René d'Harnoncourt: Indian Art of the United States; Museum of Modern Art, 2nd ed., New York, 1949.

Driver, Harold E.: Indians of North America; University of Chicago Press, Chicago, 1961.

Eggan, Fred (ed.): Social Anthropology of North American Indians; University of Chicago Press, Chicago, 1937.

Essays in Historical Anthropology of North America; Smithsonian Miscellaneous Collection, vol. 100, Washington, 1940.

Farabee, William C.: Indian Cradles; The Museum Journal, vol. 11, pp. 183–211, Philadelphia, 1920.

Hodge, F. W.: Handbook of American Indians North of Mexico; Bureau of American Ethnology, Bulletin no. 30, Washington, 1912.

Holmes, William H.: Art in Shell of the Ancient Americans; Bureau of American Ethnology, 2nd Annual Report, pp. 179–305, Washington, 1883.

Jennings, Jesse D. and Edward Norbeck (eds.): Prehistoric Man in the New World; Rice University Semicentennial Publications, Chicago, 1964.

Josephy, Alvin M., Jr. (ed.): The American Heritage Book of Indians; Simon and Schuster, New York, 1961.

Krickeberg, Walter: Das Kunstgewerbe der Eskimo und nord-amerikanischen Indianer; in: H. T. Bossert (ed.): Geschichte des Kunstgewerbes, vol. 2, pp. 154–244, Ernst Wasmuth, Berlin, 1929.

Krickeberg, Walter: Amerika; in: H. A. Bernatzik (ed.) Die Grosse Völkerkunde, vol. 3, pp. 18–258, Bibliographisches Institut, Leipzig, 1939.

Krickeberg, Walter: Ältere Ethnographica aus Nordamerika im Berliner Museum für Völkerkunde; Baessler-Archiv, new ser., vol. 3, Berlin, 1954.

Krickeberg, Walter: Die Völker Amerikas ausserhalb der Hochkulturen; in: H. Weigert: Kleine Kunstgeschichte der Welt, vol. 1, pp. 229–56, W. Kohlhammer, Stuttgart, 1956.

Krieger, Herbert W.: Aspects of Aboriginal Decorative Art in America Based on Specimens in the United States National Museum; Smithsonian Institution, Annual Report for 1930, pp. 519–56, Washington, 1931.

Kroeber, Alfred L.: Cultural and Natural Areas of Native North America; University of California Publications in Archaeology and Ethnology, vol. 38, Berkeley, 1939.

La Farge, Oliver: A Pictorial History of the American Indian; Spring Books, London, 1962.

Martin, Paul S., George I. Quimby and Donald Collier: Indians before Columbus; University of Chicago Press, Chicago, 1947.

Mason, Otis T.: Aboriginal American Basketry; U. S. National Museum, Annual Report for 1902, pp. 171–548, Washington, 1904.

Meggers, Betty J. and Clifford Evans (ed.): New Interpretations of Aboriginal American Culture History; Anthropological Society of Washington, Washington, 1955.

Miles, Charles: Indian and Eskimo Artifacts of North America; Henry Regnery, Chicago, 1963.

Monti, Franco (ed.): Le arti primitive; Capolavori nei Secoli, vol. 9, Fratelli Fabbri Editori, Milan, 1964.

Müller, Werner: Die Religionen der Indianervölker Nordamerikas; Die Religionen der Menschheit, vol. 7, pp. 171–267; W.Kohlhammer, Stuttgart, 1961.

Murdock, George P.: Ethnographic Bibliography of North America; Yale Anthropological Studies, vol. 1, New Haven, Conn., 1941; 3rd ed., 1960.

Orchard, William C.: The Technique of Porcupine-Quill Decoration among the North American Indians; Contributions from the Museum of the American Indian, Heye Foundation, vol. 4, no. 1, New York, 1916.

Orchard, William C.: Beads and Beadwork of the American Indians; Contributions from the Museum of the American Indian, Heye Foundation, vol. 11, New York, 1921.

Pericot y García, Luis: América indígena, vol. 1: El hombre americano: Los Pueblos de América; Historia de América, vol. 1, 2nd ed., Salvat Editores, Barcelona, 1962.

Schoolcraft, H. R.: Information Respecting the History, Conditions and Prospects of the Indian Tribes of the United States; Lippincott, Granbo and Co., Philadelphia, 1860.

Spencer, Robert F., Jesse D. Jennings et al.: The Native Americans; Harper and Row, New York, 1965.

Stirling, Matthew W.: Indians of the Americas; National Geographic Society, Washington, 1955.

Swanton, J. R.: The Indian Tribes of North America; Bureau of American Ethnology, Bulletin 145, Washington, 1952.

Sydow, Eckart von: Kunst und Religion der Naturvölker, Gerhard Stalling Verlag, Oldenburg, 1926.

Tschopik, Harry: Indians of North America; American Museum of Natural History, Man and Nature Publications, Science Guide no. 136, New York, 1952.

Underhill, Ruth M.: Red Man's America; University of Chicago Press, Chicago, 1953.

Vaillant, George C.: Indian Arts in North America; Harper and Brothers, New York, 1939.

West, G. A.: Tobacco, Pipes and Smoking Customs of the American Indians; Public Museum of the City of Milwaukee, Bulletin, vol. 17, nos. 1 and 2, Milwaukee, 1934.

Willey, Gordon R. (ed.): Prehistoric Settlement Patterns in the New World; Viking Fund Publications in Anthropology, no. 23, New York, 1956.

Willey, Gordon R. and Philip Phillips: Method and Theory in American Archaeology; University of Chicago Press, Chicago, 1958.

Wissler, Clark: The American Indian; 3rd ed., Oxford University Press, New York, 1938.

Wissler, Clark: Indians of the United States; Doubleday, New York, 1948.

2. EARLY SETTLEMENT

Bryan, Alan L.: Paleo-American Prehistory; Idaho State University Museum, Occasional Papers, no. 16, Pocatello, Idaho, 1965.

Butler, B. Robert: The Old Cordilleran Culture in the Pacific Northwest; Idaho State College Museum, Occasional Papers, no. 5, Pocatello, Idaho, 1961.

Sellards, Elias H.: Early Man in America; University of Texas Press, Austin, Tex., 1952.

Wormington, Hannah M.: Ancient Man in North America; The Denver Museum of Natural History, Popular Series no. 4, 4th rev. ed., Denver, Colo., 1957.

3. PETROGLYPHS

Cain, H. T.: Petroglyphs of Central Washington; University of Washington Press, Seattle, 1950.

Cressman, L. S.: Petroglyphs of Oregon; University of Oregon Monographs, Studies in Anthropology, no. 2, Eugene, Ore., 1937.

Dewdney, Selwyn and Kenneth E. Kidd: Indian Rock Paintings of the Great Lakes; Quetico Foundation Series no. 4, Toronto, Ont., 1962.

Frasetto, M. F.: A Preliminary Report on Petroglyphs in Puerto Rico; American Antiquity, vol. 25, pp. 381–91, Salt Lake City, 1960.

Gjessing, Gutorm: Petroglyphs and Pictographs in British Columbia; in: Sol Tax (ed.): Indian Tribes of Aboriginal America; Selected Papers, XXIX International Congress of Americanists, pp. 66–79, Chicago, 1952.

Heizer, Robert F. and Martin A. Baumhoff: Prehistoric Rock Art of Nevada and Eastern California; University of California Press, Berkeley and Los Angeles, 1962.

Mallery, Garrick: Pictographs of the North American Indians; Bureau of American Ethnology, 4th Annual Report, pp. 3–256, Washington, 1887.

Mallery, Garrick: Picture-writing of the American Indians; Bureau of American Ethnology, 10th Annual Report, pp. 3–807, Washington, 1893.

Perryman, Margaret: Georgia Petroglyphs; Archaeology, vol. 17, pp. 54–6, Brattleboro, Vermont, 1964.

Steward, Julian H.: Petroglyphs of California and Adjoining States; University of California Publications in American Archaeology and Ethnology, vol. 24, no. 2, Berkeley, 1929.

Steward, Julian H.: Petroglyphs of the United States; Smithsonian Institution, Annual Report for 1936, pp. 405–26, Washington, 1936.

4. THE NORTH

Bandi, Hans-Georg: Urgeschichte der Eskimo; Gustav Fischer Verlag, Stuttgart, 1965.

Birket-Smith, Kaj: Eskimoerne; Rhodos, Copenhagen, 1961.

Canadian Eskimo Art; The Department of Northern Affairs and National Resources, Ottawa, 1956.

Collins, Henry B.: Prehistoric Art of the Alaskan Eskimo; Smithsonian Miscellaneous Collection, vol. 81, no. 14, Washington, 1926.

Collins, Henry B.: Archaeology of St. Lawrence Island, Alaska; Smithsonian Miscellaneous Collection, vol. 96, no. 1, Washington, 1937.

Giddings, J. L.: The Archaeology of Bering Strait; Current Anthropology, vol. I, pp. 121–30, Chicago, 1960.

Himmelheber, Hans: Eskimokünstler; 2nd ed., Erich Röth-Verlag, Eisenach, 1953.

Hoffman, Walter J.: The Graphic Art of the Eskimos Based upon the Collections in the National Museum; U. S. National Museum, Report for 1899, pp. 739–968, Washington, 1901.

Laguna, Frederica de: The Prehistory of Northern North America as Seen from the Yukon; Society for American Archaeology, Memoir no. 12, Menasha, Wis., 1947.

Larsen, Helge and Froelich Rainey: Ipiutak and the Arctic Whale Hunting Culture; American Museum of Natural History, Anthropological Papers, vol. 42, New York, 1948.

Mason, J. Alden: Eskimo Pictorial Art; The Museum Journal, vol. 18, pp. 248–83, Philadelphia, 1927.

Meldgaard, Jørgen: Eskimo Sculpture; Methuen, London, 1960.

Ray, Dorothy J.: Artists of the Tundra and the Sea; University of Washington Press, Seattle, 1961.

Report of the Fifth Thule Expedition 1921–24; 10 vols., Gyldendalske Boghandel, Nordisk Forlag, Copenhagen, 1927–52.

5. THE NORTHWEST COAST

Adam, Leonhard: Nordwest-Amerikanische Indianerkunst; Orbis Pictus, vol. 17, Berlin, 1923.

Anonymous: Wakemap Mound. A Stratified Site on the Columbia River; Oregon Archaeological Society, Publication no. 1, Portland, Ore., 1959.

Barbeau, Marius: Totempoles; National Museum of Canada, Bulletin no. 119 (Anthropological Series no. 30), Ottawa, 1930.

Butler, B. Robert: Art at the Lower Columbia Valley; Archaeology, vol. 10, pp. 158–65, Brattleboro, Vermont, 1957.

Cressman, L. S.: Cultural Sequences at The Dalles, Oregon; American Philosophical Society, Transactions, vol. 50, part 10, Philadelphia, 1960.

Davis, Robert T.: Native Arts of the Pacific Northwest; Stanford University Press, Stanford, Calif., 1949.

Drucker, Philip: Indians of the Northwest Coast; American Museum of Natural History, Handbook Series no. 10, New York, 1955.

Emmons, George T.: The Chilkat Blanket; American Museum of Natural History, Memoirs, vol. 3, New York, 1907.

Fuhrmann, Ernst: Tlinkit und Haida; Kulturen der Erde, vol. 22, Hagen, 1922.

Garfield, Viola and A. Forest Linn: The Wolf and the Raven; University of Washington Press, Seattle, 1948.

Gunther, Erna: Northwest-Coast Indian Art; Seattle, 1962.

Hawthorn, Audrey: People of the Potlatch; Vancouver Art Gallery with the University of British Columbia; Vancouver, B. C., 1956.

Inverarity, Robert B.: Art of the Northwest Coast Indians; University of California Press, Berkeley and Los Angeles, 1950.

Krause, Aurel: Die Tlinkit Indianer; Hermann Costenoble, Jena, 1888; Eng. transl. Erna Gunther: The Tlingit Indians; American Ethnological Society, Memoir 26; Seattle, 1956.

Müller, Werner: Weltbild und Kult der Kwakiutl-Indianer; Studien zur Kulturkunde, vol. 15, Wiesbaden, 1955.

Murdock, George P.: Rank and Potlatch among the Haida; Yale University Publications in Anthropology, vol. 13, New Haven, Conn., 1936.

Olson, Ronald L.: Adze, Canoe, and House Types of the Northwest Coast; University of Washington Publications in Anthropology, vol. 2, Seattle, 1927.

Shotridge, Luis: War Helmets and Clan Hats of the Tlingit Indians; The Museum Journal, vol. 10, pp. 43–8, Philadelphia, 1919.

Shotridge, L. and F.: Indians of the Northwest; The Museum Journal, vol. 4, pp. 70–99, Philadelphia, 1913.

Strong, Emory: Prehistoric Sculpture from the Columbia River; Archaeology, vol. 14, pp. 131–37, Brattleboro, Vermont, 1961.

Strong, Emory M.: Stone Age on the Columbia River; Binfords and Mort, Portland, Ore., 1959.

Wingert, Paul S.: American Indian Sculpture: A Study of the Northwest Coast; J. J. Augustin, New York, 1949.

6. CALIFORNIA

Barrett, S. A.: Pomo Indian Basketry; University of California Publications in American Archaeology and Ethnology, vol. 7, no. 3, Berkeley, 1908.

Burnett, E. K.: Inlaid Stone and Bone Artifacts from Southern California; Contributions from the Museum of the American Indian, Heye Foundation, vol. 12, New York, 1944.

Dixon, Roland B.: Basketry Designs of the Indians of Northern California; American Museum of Natural History, Bulletin, vol. 17, no. 1, New York, 1902.

Gifford, E. W.: Californian Bone Artifacts;

University of California, Anthropological Records, vol. 3, no. 2, Berkeley and Los Angeles, 1940.

Gifford, E. W.: Californian Shell Artifacts; University of California, Anthropological Records, vol. 9, no. 1, Berkeley and Los Angeles, 1947.

Grant, Campbell: Chumash Artifacts Collected in Santa Barbara County, California; University of California Archaeological Survey, Report no. 63, pp. 1–44, Berkeley, 1964.

Heizer, Robert F.: A Bibliography of the Archaeology of California; University of California Archaeological Survey, Report no. 4, Berkeley, 1949.

Heizer, Robert F. and M. A. Whipple (ed.): The California Indians; University of California Press, Berkeley, 1951.

Kroeber, Alfred L.: Basket Designs of the Mission Indians of California; American Museum of Natural History, Anthropological Papers, vol. 20, no. 2, New York, 1922.

Kroeber, Alfred L.: Handbook of the Indians of California; Bureau of American Ethnology, Bulletin no. 78, Washington, 1925.

Merriam, C. Hart: Studies of California Indians; University of California Press, Berkeley and Los Angeles, 1955.

Merwin, B. W.: The Patty Stuart Jewett Collection; The Museum Journal, vol. 9, pp. 225–43, Philadelphia, 1918.

O'Neale, Lila M.: Yurok and Karok Basket Weavers; University of California Publications in American Archaeology and Ethnology, vol. 32, no. 1, Berkeley, 1932.

Wardle, H. Neville: A Dat-so-la-lee Basket; University Museum Bulletin, vol. 7, no. 3, pp. 12–13, Philadelphia, 1939.

7. THE SOUTHWEST

Amsden, Charles A.: Prehistoric Southwesterners from Basketmaker to Pueblo; Southwest Museum, Los Angeles, 1949.

Brew, John O.: Archaeology of Alkali Ridge, Southeastern Utah; Peabody Museum of American Archaeology and Ethnology, Harvard University, Papers, vol. 21, Cambridge, Mass., 1946.

Bunzel, Ruth L.: The Pueblo Potter; Columbia University Press, New York, 1929.

Colton, Harold S.: The Sinagua: A Summary of the Archaeology of the Region of Flagstaff, Arizona; Museum of Northern Arizona, Bulletin no. 22, Flagstaff, 1946.

Colton, Harold S.: Hopi Kachina Dolls; University of New Mexico, Albuquerque, 1949.

Colton, Harold S.: (ed.): Ceramic Series; Museum of Northern Arizona, Flagstaff, 1952ff.

Colton, Harold S. and L. L. Hargrave: Handbook of Northern Arizona Pottery Wares; Museum of Northern Arizona, Bulletin no. 11, Flagstaff, 1937.

Dockstader, Frederick J.: The Kachina and the White Man; Cranbrook Institute of Science, Bulletin no. 35, Bloomfield Hills, Mich., 1954.

Fewkes, J. W.: Antiquities of the Mesa Verde National Park: Cliff Palace; Bureau of American Ethnology, Bulletin no. 51, Washington, 1911.

Foster, Kenneth E.: Navajo Sandpaintings; Navajoland Publications, 3rd series, Navajo Tribal Museum, Window Rock, Arizona, n.d.

Gifford, E. W.: Pottery Making in the Southwest; University of California Publications in American Archaeology and Ethnology, vol. 23, no. 8, Berkeley, 1928.

Gladwin, Harold S.: A History of the Ancient Southwest; Portland, Me., 1957.

Gladwin, Harold S., Emil W. Haury, E. B. Sayles and Nora Gladwin: Excavations at Snaketown I: Material Culture; Medallion Papers, no. 25, Globe, Ariz., 1937.

Hawley, Florence M.: Field Manual of Prehistoric Southwestern Pottery types; University of New Mexico, Anthropological Series, Bulletin no. 291, vol. 1, no. 4, Albuquerque, N. M., 1936.

Herold, Joyce: Prehistoric Settlement and Physical Environment in the Mesa Verde Area; University of Utah Anthropological Papers, no. 53, Salt Lake City, 1961.

Hibben, Frank C.: Prehispanic Paintings at Pottery Mound; Archaeology, vol. 13, pp. 267–74, Brattleboro, Vt., 1960.

Hunt, W. Ben: Kachina Dolls; Milwaukee Public Museum, Popular Science Handbook Series, no. 7, Milwaukee, 1957.

Kidder, Alfred V.: An Introduction to the Study of Southwestern Archaeology; new ed. [with a Summary of Southwestern Archaeology Today by Irving Rouse], Yale

University Press, New Haven and London, 1962.

McGregor, John C.: Southwestern Archaeology; rev. ed., University of Illinois Press, Urbana, 1965.

Marriott, Alice: Maria the Potter of San Ildefonso; University of Oklahoma Press, Norman, 1948.

Martin, Paul S. and E. S. Willis: Anasazi Painted Pottery in the Field Museum of Natural History; Field Museum of Natural History, Anthropological Memoirs, vol. 5, Chicago, 1940.

Morris, Earl H. and R. F. Burgh: Anasazi Basketry, Basket Maker II through Pueblo III; Carnegie Institution of Washington, Publication no. 533, Washington, 1941.

Morris, Earl H. and Robert F. Burgh: Basket Maker II Sites near Durango, Colorado; Carnegie Institution of Washington, Publication no. 604, Washington, 1954.

Parsons, Elsie C.: Pueblo Indian Religion; University of Chicago Press, Chicago, 1939.

Pepper, G. H.: Pueblo Bonito; American Museum of Natural History, Anthropological Papers, vol. 27, New York, 1920.

Reichard, Gladys and Frank J. Newcomb: Shooting Chant: Sandpaintings of the Navajo; J. J. Augustin, New York, 1937.

Roberts, Frank H. H.: Shabik'eshchee Village: A Late Basketmaker Site in the Chaco Canyon, New Mexico; Bureau of American Ethnology, Bulletin no. 92, Washington, 1929.

Sayles, E. B. and Ernst Antevs: The Cochise Culture; Medallion Papers, no. 24, Globe, Ariz., 1941.

Schroeder, Albert H.: The Hohokam, Sinagua and the Hakataya; Archives of Archaeology, no. 5; Madison, Wis., 1960.

Smith, Watson: Kiva Mural Decorations at Awátovi and Kawaika-a; Peabody Museum of American Archaeology and Ethnology, Harvard University, Papers, vol. 37, Cambridge, Mass., 1952.

Stevenson, Matilda C.: The Zuñi Indians; Bureau of American Ethnology, 23rd Annual Report, pp. 1–634, Washington, 1902.

Stubbs, Stanley A.: A Bird's-Eye View of the Pueblos; University of Oklahoma Press, Norman, 1950.

Underhill, Ruth M.: The Navajos; The Civilization of the American Indian Series, no. 43, University of Oklahoma Press, Norman, 1958.

Wheat, Joe Ben: Mogollon Culture Prior to A.D. 1000; American Anthropological Association, Memoir no. 82, Menasha, Wis., 1955.

Wheelwright, Mary C.: Hail Chant and Water Chant; Navajo Religion Series, vol. 2, Museum of Navajo Ceremonial Art, Santa Fé, N.M., 1946.

Wormington, Hannah M.: Prehistoric Indians of the Southwest; Denver Museum of Natural History, Popular Series, no. 7, 3rd ed., Denver, Colo., 1956.

Wyman, Leland C. (ed.): Beautyway: A Navajo Ceremonial; Bollingen Series, no. 53, Pantheon Books, New York, 1957.

8. THE GREAT PLAINS

Catlin, George: Illustrations of Manners, Customs and Conditions of the North American Indian, New York, 1841.

Feder, Norman: Art of the Eastern Plains Indians; The Nathan Sturges Jarvis Collection, Guide no. 2, The Brooklyn Museum, Brooklyn, N. Y., 1964.

Fletcher, Alice C. and Francis La Fleche: The Omaha Tribe; Bureau of American Ethnology, 27th Annual Report, pp. 15–654, Washington, 1906.

Hall, H. V.: Some Shields of the Plains and Southwest; The Museum Journal, vol. 17, pp. 36–61, Philadelphia, 1926.

Hartmann, Horst: George Catlin and Balduin Möllhausen: Zwei Interpreten der Indianer und des Alten Westens, Baessler-Archiv, new ser., supp. fasc. no. 3, Berlin, 1963.

Hotz, Gottfried: Indianische Ledermalereien; Dietrich Reimer, Berlin, 1960.

Kroeber, Alfred L.: Decorative Symbolism of the Arapaho; American Anthropologist, new ser., vol. 3, 1901.

Laubin, Reginald and Gladys: The Indian Tipi; University of Oklahoma Press, Norman, 1957.

Lowie, Robert H.: Crow Indian Art; American Museum of Natural History, Anthropological Papers, vol. 21, no. 4, New York, 1922.

Lowie, Robert H.: Indians of the Plains; McGraw-Hill, New York, 1954.

Roe, Frank G.: The Indian and the Horse; University of Oklahoma Press, Norman, 1955.

Vatter, Ernst: Historienmalerei und heraldische Bilderschrift der nordamerikanischen Präriestämme; Jahrbuch für Prähistorische und Ethnographische Kunst, vol. 3, pp. 46–81, Leipzig, 1927.

Wedel, Waldo R.: Prehistoric Man on the Great Plains; University of Oklahoma Press, Norman, 1961.

Wied, Maximilian Prinz zu: Reise in das Innere Nordamerikas in den Jahren 1832–1834; Koblenz, 1839–41.

Wildschut, William and John C. Ewers: Crow Indian Beadwork; Contributions from the Museum of the American Indian, Heye Foundation, vol. 16, New York, 1959.

Wissler, Clark: Decorative Art of the Sioux Indians; American Museum of Natural History, Bulletin, vol. 18, no. 3, New York, 1904.

Wissler, Clark: Ceremonial Bundles of the Blackfoot Indians; American Museum of Natural History, Anthropological Papers, vol. 7, no. 2, New York, 1912.

Wissler, Clark: Structural Basis to the Decoration of Costumes among the Plains Indians; American Museum of Natural History, Anthropological Papers, vol. 17, no. 3, New York, 1916.

Wissler, Clark: Distribution of Mocassin Decorations among the Plains Tribes; American Museum of Natural History, Anthropological Papers, vol. 29, no. 1, New York, 1927.

Wissler, Clark: North American Indians of the Plains; American Museum of Natural History, Handbook Series, no. 1, 3rd ed., New York, 1941.

9. THE NORTHEAST

Byers, Douglas S.: The Eastern Archaic: Some Problems and Hypotheses; American Antiquity, vol. 24, pp. 233–56, Salt Lake City, 1959.

Deuel, Thorne: Hopewellian Communities in Illinois; Illinois State Museum, Scientific Papers, vol. 5, Springfield, 1952.

Eyman, Frances: An Unusual Winnebago War Club and an American Water Monster; Expedition, vol. 5, no. 4, pp. 31–35, Philadelphia, 1963.

Eyman, Frances: Lacrosse and the Cayuga Thunder Rite; Expedition, vol. 6, no. 4, pp. 14–19, Philadelphia, 1964.

Fenton, William N.: Masked Medicine Societies of the Iroquois; Smithsonian Institution, Annual Report for 1940, pp. 397–430, Washington, 1941.

Fenton, William N. and J. Gulick (eds.): Symposium on Cherokee and Iroquois Culture; Bureau of American Ethnology, Bulletin no. 180, Washington, 1961.

Ford, J. A. and Gordon W. Willey: An Interpretation of the Prehistory of the Eastern United States; American Anthropologist, vol. 43, pp. 325–63, Menasha, Wis., 1941.

Griffin, James B. (ed.): Archaeology of the Eastern United States; University of Chicago Press, Chicago, 1952.

Holmes, William H.: Aboriginal Pottery of the Eastern United States; Bureau of American Ethnology, 20th Annual Report, pp. 1–237, Washington, 1899.

Jenks, A. E.: The Wild Rice Gatherers of the Upper Great Lakes; Bureau of American Ethnology, 19th Annual Report, part 2, pp. 1013–137, Washington, 1898.

Johnson, Frederick (ed.): Man in Northeastern North America; Robert S. Peabody Foundation for Archaeology, Papers, vol. 3, Andover, Mass., 1946.

Moorehead, Warren K.: The Hopewell Mound Group of Ohio; Field Museum of Natural History, Anthropological Series, vol. 6, no. 5, Chicago, 1922.

Morgan, Lewis H.: League of the Ho-de-no-sau-nee or Iroquois; Rochester, N.Y., 1851.

Müller, Werner: Die Religionen der Waldlandindianer Nordamerikas; Dietrich Reimer, Berlin, 1956.

Quimby, George L.: Indian Life in the Upper Great Lakes; University of Chicago Press, Chicago, 1960.

Ritchie, William A.: Indian History of New York State, Part II: The Iroquoian Tribes; New York State Museum, Educational Leaflet Series, no. 7, Albany, N.Y., 1953.

Ritchie, William A.: An Introduction to Hudson Valley Prehistory; New York State Museum and Science Service, Bulletin no. 367, Albany, N.Y., 1958.

Ritchie, William A.: Indian History of New York State, Part III: The Algonquian

Tribes; New York State Museum and Science Service, Albany, N.Y., n.d.

Ritzenthaler, Robert (ed.): The Old Copper Culture of Wisconsin; The Wisconsin Archaeologist, vol. 38, no. 4; Lake Mills, Wis., 1957.

Rowe, Chandler W.: The Effigy Mound Culture of Wisconsin; Milwaukee Public Museum Publications in Anthropology, no. 3, Milwaukee, 1956.

Shetrone, H. C.: The Mound Builders; D. Appleton, New York, 1930.

Speck, Frank G.: Huron Moose Hair Embroidery; American Anthropologist, vol. 13, pp. 1–14, Lancaster, Pa., 1911.

Speck, Frank G.: The Double-Curve Motive in Northeastern Algonkin Art; Canada Department of Mines, Geological Survey, Memoir no. 42 (Anthropological Series, no. 1), Ottawa, 1914.

Speck, Frank G,: Symbolism in Penobscot Art; American Museum of Natural History, Anthropological Papers, vol. 29, no. 2, New York, 1927.

Speck, Frank G.: Naskapi; University of Oklahoma Press, Norman, 1935.

Speck, Frank G.: Montagnais Art in Birchbark: A Circumpolar Trait; Museum of the American Indian, Heye Foundation, Indian Notes and Monographs, vol. 11, no. 2, New York, 1937.

Speck, Frank G.: Concerning Iconology and the Masking Complex in Eastern North America; University Museum Bulletin, vol. 15, no. 1, Philadelphia, 1950.

Speck, Frank G. and W. C. Orchard: The Penn Wampum Belts; Museum of the American Indian, Heye Foundation, Leaflet no. 4, New York, 1925.

Willoughby, Charles C.: The Art of the Great Earthwork Builders of Ohio; Smithsonian Institution, Annual Report for 1916, pp. 489–500, Washington, 1917.

Willoughby, Charles C.: Antiquities of the New England Indians; Peabody Museum of American Archaeology and Ethnology, Cambridge, Mass., 1935.

10. THE SOUTHEAST

Burnett, E. K.: The Spiro Mound Collection in the Museum; Contributions from the Museum of the American Indian, Heye Foundation, vol. 14, New York, 1945.

Caldwell, Joseph R.: Trend and Tradition in the Prehistory of the Eastern United States; Illinois State Museum, Scientific Papers, vol. 10, Springfield, 1958.

Cushing, Frank H.: Exploration of Ancient Key Dwellers' Remains on the Gulf Coast of Florida; American Philosophical Society, Proceedings, vol. 35, pp. 329–432, Philadelphia, 1897.

Fairbanks, Charles H.: Archaeology of the Funeral Mound, Ocmulgee National Monument, Georgia; National Park Service, Archaeological Research Series, no. 3, Washington, 1956.

Ford, James A. and George I. Quimby: The Tchefuncte Culture: An Early Occupation of the Lower Mississippi Valley; Society for American Archaeology, Memoir no. 2, Menasha, Wis., 1945.

Fundaburk, Emma Lila and Mary Douglas Foreman: Sun Circles and Human Hands; Luverne, Ala., 1957.

Griffin, John W. (ed.): The Florida Indian and His Neighbors; Inter-American Center, Rollins College, Winter Park, Fla., 1949.

Kellar, James H., A. R. Kelly and Edward V. McMichael: The Mandeville Site in Southwestern Georgia; American Antiquity, vol. 27, pp. 336–55, Salt Lake City, 1962.

Kelly, A. R. and Lewis H. Larson, Jr.: Explorations at Etowah, Georgia; Archaeology, vol. 10, pp. 39–48, Brattleboro, Vt., 1957.

Lewis, Thomas M. N. and Madeline Kneberg: Tribes that Slumber; University of Tennessee Press, Knoxville, Tenn., 1960.

Merwin, B. W.: Basketry of the Chitimacha Indians; Museum Journal, vol. 10, pp. 29–34, Philadelphia, 1919.

Mooney, James: Myths of the Cherokee; Bureau of American Ethnology, 19th Annual Report, part 1, pp. 3-576, Washington, 1900.

Phillips, Philip, James A. Ford and James B. Griffin: Archaeological Survey in the Lower Mississippi Alluvial Valley, 1940–1947; Peabody Museum of American Archaeology and Ethnology, Harvard University, Papers, vol. 25, Cambridge, Mass., 1951.

Speck, Frank G.: Decorative Art and Basketry of the Cherokee, Public Museum of the City of Milwaukee, Bulletin, vol. 2, no. 2, Milwaukee, 1920.

Swanton, John R.: The Indians of the South-eastern United States; Bureau of American Ethnology, Bulletin no. 137, Washington, 1946.

Waring, Antonio and Preston Holder: A Pre-historic Ceremonial Complex in the South-eastern United States; American Anthro-pologist, vol. 47, pp. 1–34, Washington, 1945.

Willey, Gordon R.: Archaeology of the Florida Gulf Coast; Smithsonian Institution Mis-cellaneous Collection, vol. 113, Washing-ton, 1949.

11. THE WEST INDIES

Bullen, Ripley P.: The Archaeology of Grenada, West Indies; Contributions of the Florida State Museum, Social Sciences, no. 11; Gainesville, Fla., 1964.

Bullen, Ripley P.: The Archaeology of Grenada, West Indies, and the Spread of Ceramic People into the West Indies; Actas del 36° Congreso Internacional de Ameri-canistas [in press].

Dockstader, Frederick J.: Indian Art in Middle America; New York Graphic Society, Greenwich, Conn., 1964.

Granberry, Julian: The Cultural Position of the Bahamas in Caribbean Archaeology; American Antiquity, vol. 22, pp. 128–34, Salt Lake City, 1956.

Harrington, M. R.: Cuba before Columbus; Museum of the American Indian, Heye Foundation, Indian Notes and Mono-graphs, New York, 1921.

Lovén, Sven: Über die Wurzeln der Tainischen Kultur; Gothenburg, 1924.

Rouse, Irving et al.: The West-Indies; Bureau of American Ethnology, Handbook of the South American Indians, Bulletin no. 143, vol. 4, pp. 495–565, Washington, 1948.

Rouse, Irving: Areas and Periods of Culture in the Greater Antilles; Southwestern Jour-nal of Anthropology, vol. 7, pp. 248–65, Albuquerque, N.M., 1951.

Rouse, Irving: The Entry of Man into the West Indies; Yale University Publications in Anthropology, no. 61, New Haven, Conn., 1960.

MAPS

The maps include only tribes and sites that are mentioned in the text or that are of special importance. They were drawn by Frédéric Barault, Athens, following sketches provided by the author.

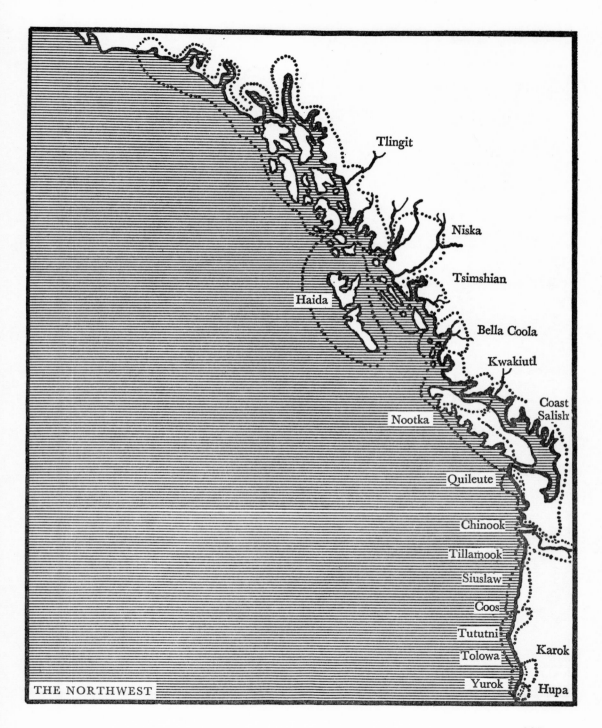

Tlingit

Niska

Tsimshian

Haida

Bella Coola

Kwakiutl

Coast Salish

Nootka

Quileute

Chinook

Tillamook

Siuslaw

Coos

Tututni

Tolowa

Karok

Yurok

Hupa

THE NORTHWEST

221

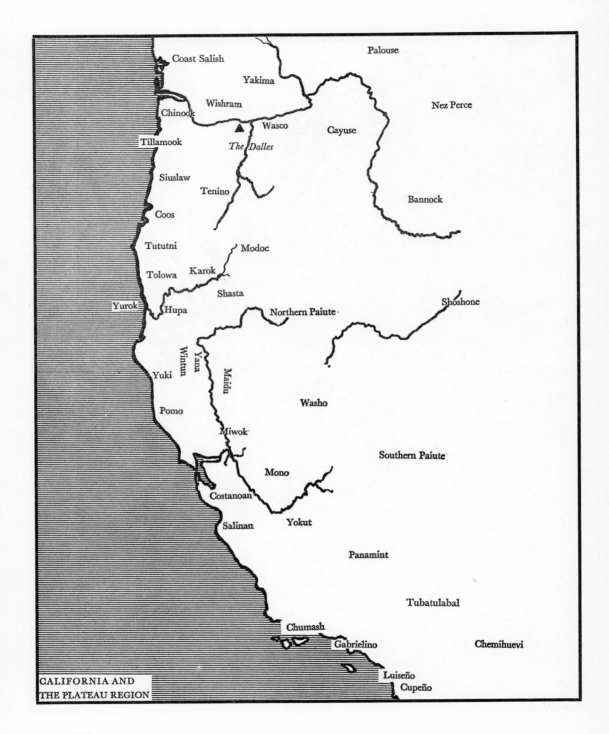

CALIFORNIA AND
THE PLATEAU REGION

Coast Salish

Palouse

Yakima

Wishram

Nez Perce

Chinook

Wasco

Cayuse

Tillamook

The Dalles

Siuslaw

Tenino

Bannock

Coos

Tututni

Modoc

Tolowa

Karok

Shasta

Shoshone

Yurok

Hupa

Northern Paiute

Yuki

Wintun

Yana

Maidu

Washo

Pomo

Miwok

Southern Paiute

Costanoan

Mono

Salinan

Yokut

Panamint

Tubatulabal

Chumash

Gabrielino

Chemihuevi

Luiseño

Cupeño

222

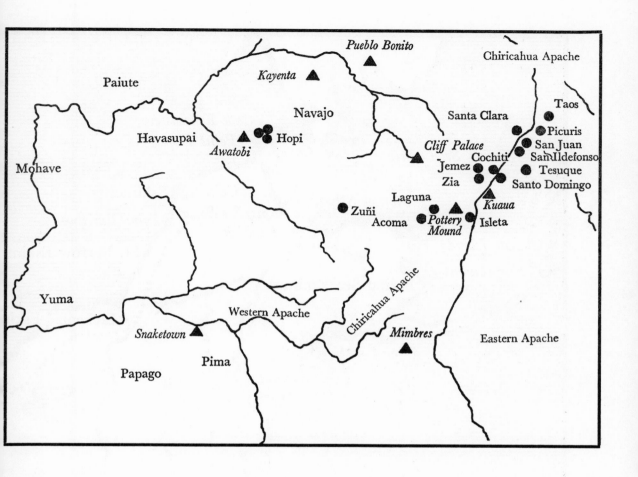

THE SOUTHWEST

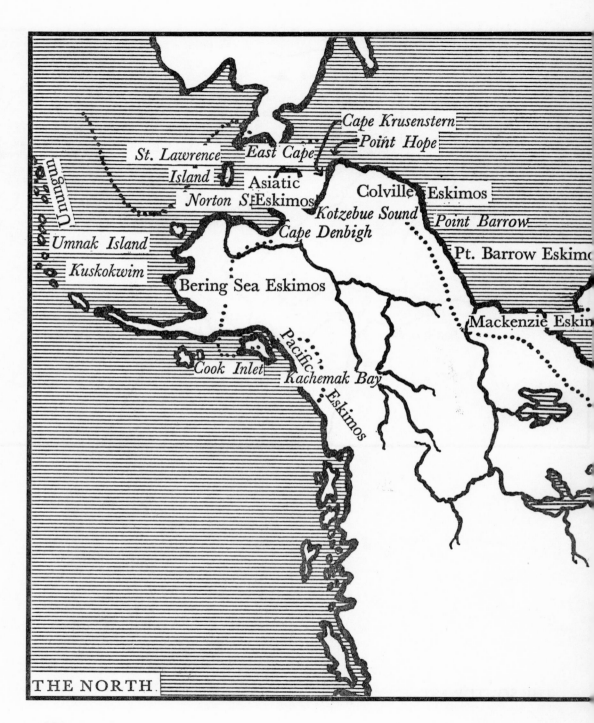

Cape Krusenstern

Point Hope

St. Lawrence
Island

East Cape

Asiatic

Colville Eskimos

Point Barrow

Ungunun

Norton S.t Eskimos

Kotzebue Sound

Cape Denbigh

Pt. Barrow Eskimo

Umnak Island

Kuskokwim

Bering Sea Eskimos

Mackenzie Eskim

Pacific

Cook Inlet

Kachemak Bay

Eskimos

THE NORTH.

224

Polar
Eskimos

Angmagssalik

West Greenland Eskimos

Baffinland Eskimos

Igulik

per

mos

Netsilik

Caribou Eskimos

Labrador

Eskimos

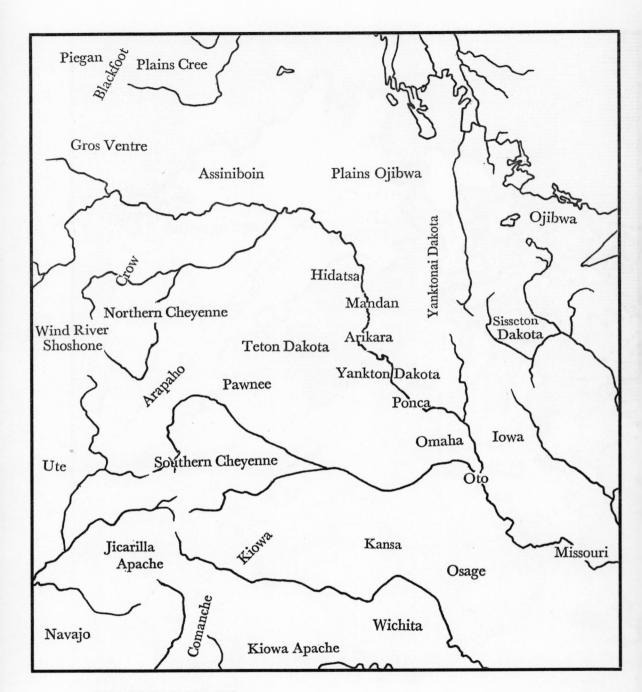

THE GREAT PLAINS

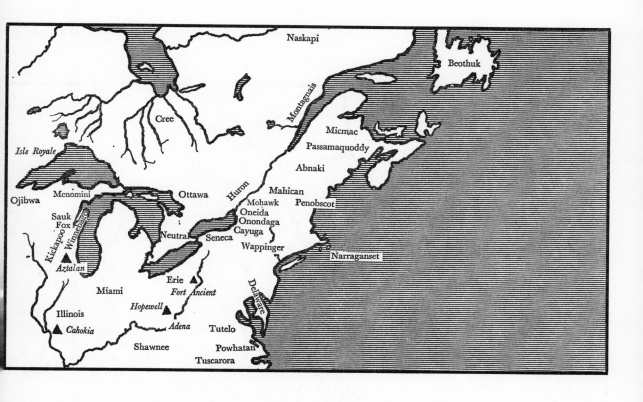

THE NORTHEAST

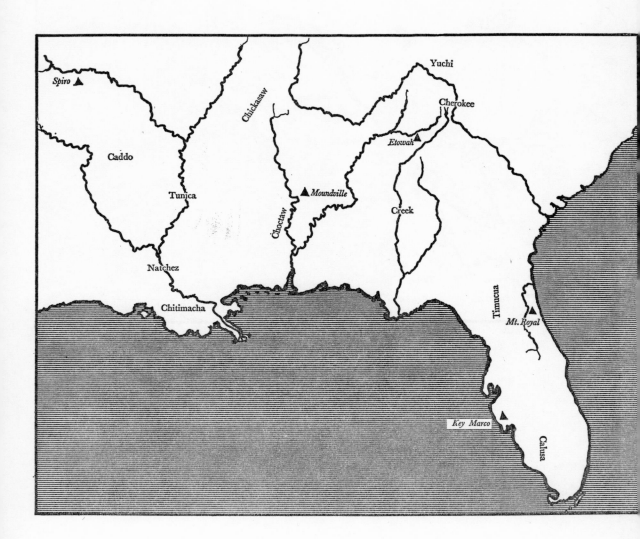

THE SOUTHEAST

228

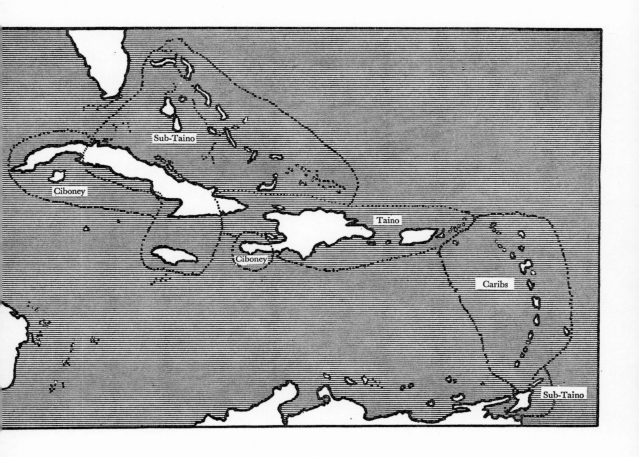

Sub-Taino

Ciboney

Ciboney

Taino

Caribs

Sub-Taino

THE WEST INDIES

CHRONOLOGICAL CHARTS

CHART I

Chief periods and phases of Eskimo archaeology. After Bandi, 1965; Collins, in Jennings and Norbeck, 1964; and Giddings, 1960.

CHART II

Chief archaeological periods of the Southwest.

CHART III

Archaeological phases and complexes of the Northeast. This chart shows how complicated such schemas can be, even when the data are presented in highly compressed form. After Griffin, in Jennings and Norbeck, 1964.

CHART IV

Archaeological phases of the West Indies. After Bullen, 1964 and n.d.; Granberry, 1956; Rouse, 1951 and 1960.

CHART V

Development and influences of various traditions of the pre-Columbian Southeast. After Caldwell, 1958.

Date	Southern Alaska	St. Lawrence Island	Amer. side of Bering Strait	North-western Alaska	North-eastern Canada Hudson Bay	North Greenland	West Greenland
1800 A.D.	modern		modern	modern	modern	modern	modern
1600 A.D.			Nukleet III				Inugsuk
1400 A.D.	Kachemak Bay III	Thule-Punuk	Nukleet II	Western Thule	Thule	Thule	×
1200 A.D.	×	×	×				Thule
1000 A.D.	Kachemak Bay II	Punuk	Nukleet I	×			
800 A.D.		×		Birnirk			
600 A.D.		Early Punuk					
400 A.D.	×	× Old Bering Sea III		Ipiutak			Dorset
200 A.D.	Kachemak Bay I	× Old Bering Sea II			Dorset	Dorset	
0		× Okvik II	Norton	Near-Ipiutak?			
200 B.C.		×					
400 B.C.		Okvik I					Sarqaq
600 B.C.						Independence II	
800 B.C.			×	Choris			
1000 B.C.							
1400 B.C.				Old Whaling?		×	
1800 B.C.							
2200 B.C.			Denbigh Flint Complex	Denbigh Flint Complex	Sarqaq	Independence I	

CHRONOLOGICAL CHART II

Date	Mogollon	Hohokam	Anasazi	Hakataya	Utah
1700 A.D.			Historic Pueblo		
1500 A.D.			Regressive Pueblo		
1300 A.D.		Classic stage	Great Pueblo		
1100 A.D.	Mogollon V	Sedentary stage			
	Mogollon IV			Patayan / Sinagua / Cohonina	Freemont
900 A.D.			Developmental Pueblo		
700 A.D.	Mogollon III	Colonial stage			
500 A.D.	Mogollon II		Modified Basketmaker		
300 A.D.		Pioneer stage			
100 A.D.	Mogollon I		Basketmaker		
100 B.C.					
300 B.C.					
500 B.C.					
700 B.C.					
	San Pedro	San Pedro			

233

CHRONOLOGICAL CHART III

Date	Period	Missouri	Iowa	Minnesota	Wisconsin	Illinois	Michigan
	Late Woodland / Mississippi	Utz-Oneota	Orr-Oneota	Blue Earth / Black Duck II	Bell / Lake Winnebago / Grand River	Fisher / Trappist – Spoon River / Kincaid	Moccasin Bluff
				Cambria			Missaukee
1000 A.D.		Steed-Kisker / Sterns Creek	Mill Creek / Effigy Mound	Black Duck I	Aztalan / Effigy Mound / Kalterman	Old Village / Raymond	Spring Creek
		Boone				Jersey Bluff	Brooks
	Middle Woodland	Kansas City Hopewell	Harpers Ferry	Rainy River / Howard Lake	Red Cedar River / Trempealeau Hopewell	Baehr Hopewell	Norton Hopewell / Killarney Bay
I A.D.						Havana	
	Early Woodland			Lamoille		Morton / Crab Orchard / Red Ochre	Andrews
1000 B.C.					Osceola / Reigh		Menominee / Glacial Kame / Riverto
	Archaic Hunters and Plant Gatherers — Late			Old Copper / Minnesota »Man«	Durst		Old Copper / Feeheley
2000 B.C.							Dustin
					Raddatz		
4000 B.C.	Middle	Nebo Hill	Turin	Browns Valley		Hidden Valley / Faulkner (?)	
		Research Cave I				Modoc I	
5000 B.C.	Early				Renier		Satchell Comple
6000 B.C.							Hi-Lo
	Palaeo-Indian Period	Dalton / Graham Cave I	Quimby		Early Raddatz		Holcombe
8000 B.C.							Dobbelaar / Barnes

←——— Hunters with channelled stone poir

234

CHRONOLOGICAL CHART III

Indiana	West Virginia Ohio	Ontario	Pennsylvania New York	New England	New Jersey	Date
	Madisonville Whittlesey	Pic River Huron-Iroquois	New York Iroquois	Clarks Pond Titicult		
Angel		Uren	Monongahela		Rosenkrans Ferry	
	Fort Ancient		Owasco			
ˮounge Albee		Pic River I	Clemsons Island Oaklawn			1000 A.D.
Yankeetown	Newtown		Point Peninsula III			
La Motte						
Mann Late Adena	Intrusive Mound Culture Hopewell	Le Vesconte Serpent Mound	North Beach Point Peninsula II	Locust Spring	Abbott Farm	1 A.D.
	Adena					
Petersen			Meadowood (Point Peninsula I)		Skunk Run	
		Picton	Transitional	Late Boreal	Red Valley	1000 B.C.
		Old Copper	Late Laurentian		Koens-Crispin	
Du Bois		Malcolm I	Lamoka	Early »Boreal«		2000 B.C.
	Raisch-Smith Rohr I	Early Laurentian	Bare Island	Boylston Wapanucket I Kelley (?)		4000 B.C.
	Sawmill					5000 B.C.
	McConnell					6000 B.C.
		Brohm Sheguindah I George Lake	Reagan	Twin Rivers Bull Brook		8000 B.C.

most areas of the Northeast ———→

CHRONOLOGICAL CHART IV

Periods	Date	Western Cuba	Central Cuba	Eastern Cuba	Central Bahamas	Northern Bahamas	Turks and Caicos Islands	Jamaica
IV	1500 A.D.			Pueblo Viejo / Carrier?	Carrier?	Meillac	Carrier	Bani?
			Bani		Meillac		Meillac	
III b	1000 A.D.	Cayo Redondo and Guayabo Blanco		Bani				
III a	700 A.D.		Cayo Redondo and Guayabo Blanco	Cayo Redondo and Guayabo Blanco				
II b	300 A.D.							
II a	0							
I	1000 B.C.							

Caribs

Taino

Arawak

Pre-Arawak

Pre-ceramic units

CHRONOLOGICAL CHART IV

Haiti	Dominican Republic	Western Puerto Rico	Eastern Puerto Rico	Virgin Islands	Martinique	Sta. Lucia	Grenada	Trinidad
				A		Fannis	Savanne Suazey	
Carrier	Boca Chica	Capa?	Esperanza				Westerhall	Bontour
				Magens Bay		Choc		
Meillac			Santa Elena	B	Paquemar			
		Ostiones					Caliviny	Erin
Macady	Anadel		Ostiones	C		Massacre		
Couri and Cabaret	Rail Road Cave	Cuevas	Cuevas	Late Coral Bay	La Salle	Troumasee B	Salt Pond	Palo Seco
						Troumasee A	Pearls	
		Corozo and Loiza	Hacienda Grande	Early Coral Bay			Black Point	Cedros
		Corozo and Loiza		Krum Bay				Ortoire

237

CHRONOLOGICAL CHART V

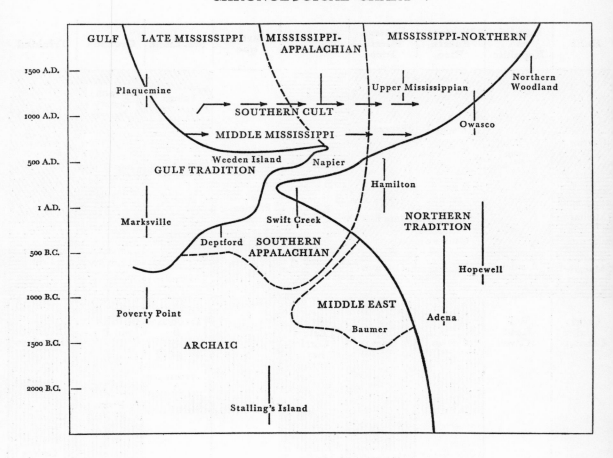

Traditions (capitals) and important periods (lower case) in the south-eastern United States showing their chronological and geographical development. The vertical space indicates time, the horizontal one regional distribution, with south to the left and north to the right. The two solid lines demarcate two of the most important traditions: Gulf in the south (left) and Northern (right), the latter embracing, among others, the Adena and Hopewell periods. The vertical strokes indicate length of time. As the curves indicate, in the first half of the first millennium of the Christian era the Northern tradition pushed far to the south, later pulling back again, while the influence of the Gulf tradition advanced northwards. Between these two traditions lies the territory of the Southern Appalachian tradition, which is delimited by a broken line. Despite strong foreign influences during the first millennium this tradition firmly established itself again. By contrast, the Archaic stage and the Middle Eastern tradition did not survive into the Christian era. Towards the end of the first millennium and about A.D. 1400 two complexes, the Middle Mississippi and the Southern Cult (horizontal arrows), advanced northwards, where they influenced the Sedentary traditions, though without creating well-defined cultural units. At the time of the European conquest of the Southeast the traditions shown at the top of the chart were dominant.

238

SOURCES OF COLOUR PLATES

COLOUR PHOTOGRAPHS

Those plates not mentioned here were generously supplied by the museums.

INDEX

The numerals in italics refer to the plates and figures